Corporate Acquisitions and Mergers in New Zealand

Corporate Acquisitions and Mergers in New Zealand

Jennifer Coote

Bell Gully

This book was originally published as a chapter in Corporate Acquisitions and Mergers.

General Editor: Peter Begg

Wolters Kluwer

Published by:
Kluwer Law International B.V.
PO Box 316
2400 AH Alphen aan den Rijn
The Netherlands
E-mail: international-sales@wolterskluwer.com
Website: lrus.wolterskluwer.com

Sold and distributed by:
Wolters Kluwer Legal & Regulatory U.S.
7201 McKinney Circle
Frederick, MD 21704
United States of America
Email: customer.service@wolterskluwer.com

ISBN 978-94-035-3022-2

e-Book: ISBN 978-94-035-2983-7
web-PDF: ISBN 978-94-035-2984-4

Contents

Bell Gully

Bell Gully is New Zealand's leading law firm. Bell Gully's team of lawyers combines market-leading corporate and commercial, financial services, dispute resolution, property and tax capability along with a wide array of specialist skills. Bell Gully is consistently ranked in the world's most reputable and respected legal directories at the top of their ranking tables. Bell Gully has a track record of winning major legal awards, in recognition of the firm's achievements and for the excellent and innovative legal work undertaken with its clients.

Bell Gully works on diverse projects with many leading New Zealand and international companies. As one of the oldest firms in New Zealand, established in 1840, Bell Gully has served some domestic clients since the 1800s and its lawyers were instrumental in setting up some of New Zealand's most well-known businesses.

Bell Gully is globally connected with networks throughout the world with leading law firms, business advisory firms, investment advisers, regulators and companies. Bell Gully advises a number of offshore clients with interests in New Zealand and has a growing practice advising private investors on their New Zealand based investments.

Author

Jennifer is an experienced corporate transactions lawyer, with experience in New Zealand and London. She advises on private mergers and acquisitions, joint venture arrangements and equity capital markets transactions.

Clients seek Jennifer out for transactions in a wide range of industries including financial services, manufacturing and industrial, technology and telecommunications, and she advises corporates, private equity and sovereign wealth funds on both the buy and sell sides.

Jennifer is focused on assisting clients with delivering complex transactions in a timely manner and providing commercially focused and pragmatic advice. She has been ranked in leading directories as a 'rising star' and 'next generation' and is described as 'highly capable'.

This publication is necessarily general in nature. You should seek professional advice before taking any action in relation to the matters dealt with in this publication.

1 INTRODUCTION TO NEW ZEALAND

1.1 Overview

[01] Geographically isolated in the South Pacific, New Zealand has overcome its distance from major markets to make the most of its advantages. The result is a diverse economy, with strong trade relationships with Australia, China, the United Kingdom (UK), the European Union, the United States, and Japan, among others.

[02] In 2020 the country's population reached five million, after recording the fastest addition of a million people in New Zealand's history. Growth has been driven in equal parts by a natural increase and strong net migration, resulting in a blend of cultures that includes the indigenous Māori population, New Zealand European population, and growing populations of Asian and Pacific peoples. There are three official languages: English, te reo Māori, and New Zealand Sign Language.

[03] New Zealand has enjoyed positive economic growth for most of the past three-and-a-half decades.[1] The country also sustains a robust labour market, with a highly skilled and educated workforce. Since 2005, the unemployment rate has consistently been below the Organisation for Economic Co-operation and Development (OECD) average.[2]

1.2 Government and Political System

[04] New Zealand is considered as one of the world's most stable democracies. The House of Representatives is elected using the mixed member proportional representation (MMP) voting system. Political parties are represented in proportion to the share of the party vote their party secures in general elections, held every three years. Since it was adopted in a binding referendum in 1993, MMP has resulted in stable coalition governments usually formed by two or more political parties. Four of the last five governments have each been three-term governments that have remained in power for nine years.

[05] New Zealand's head of State is Queen Elizabeth II, represented in New Zealand by the Governor General, and by convention, the sovereign acts on the advice of Government in all but the most exceptional circumstances. New Zealand has no written constitution; instead, its system of Government works through a

1 NZ Story, *Open for Business: The Case for Investing in New Zealand*, p. 3, https://toolkit.nzstory.govt.nz/assets/182833 (accessed 22 Aug. 2020).

2 Ministry of Business Innovation and Employment, *Our Employment Strategy: Everyone Working to Deliver a Productive, Sustainable and Inclusive New Zealand*, p. 2, https://www.mbie.govt.nz/dmsdocument/6614 (accessed 22 Aug. 2020).

number of acts of Parliament, common law and a number of unwritten constitutional conventions. New Zealand's Parliament is unicameral, with a single chamber, and there are no federal laws.

[06] The Treaty of Waitangi (the *Treaty*), signed between the Crown and a number of Māori chiefs in 1840, plays an important role in New Zealand. Among the key principles in the Treaty are promises to protect Māori culture and to enable it to continue in New Zealand. The Waitangi Tribunal, which was established in 1975, enables claims to be made and settlements for historical breaches of the Treaty are negotiated by the Crown, through the Office of Treaty Settlements.

1.3 Legal System

[07] New Zealand is a common law jurisdiction, modelled on the UK's legal system, reflecting its heritage and position as a member of the Commonwealth. The law in New Zealand is developed from the decisions of the courts and legislative statutes enacted by the New Zealand Parliament, with reference to relevant case law from other Commonwealth countries, particularly the UK and Australia.

[08] New Zealand has two types of courts, general and specialist. General courts consist of four levels: the District Court, High Court, Court of Appeal and Supreme Court. The Supreme Court was established in 2004, replacing the Judicial Committee of the Privy Council of the UK as the highest court in New Zealand. Specialist courts deal with specific areas of the law, for example, the Environment Court deals with resource management, planning and development matters.

[09] The judiciary and sit alongside Parliament and the executive (the Governor General, the Prime Minister, Cabinet and government departments) to form the three branches of government. Each branch works independently from the other based on the principle of the 'separation of powers'. Under the rule of law, all individuals including government are subject to the law and have the right to an independent and impartial judiciary.

[10] Ranked 7th of 128 countries and jurisdictions in the World Justice Project Rule of Law Index 2020,[3] and 1st in the East Asia and Pacific region, there is strong adherence to the law in New Zealand. In the same index, New Zealand is ranked 5th for regulatory enforcement. Another international survey, the World Bank's Doing Business 2020, ranks New Zealand 23rd out of 133 countries for contract enforcement when taking into account the time and cost of resolving a commercial dispute and the quality of judicial processes.[4]

[3] World Justice Project, *World Justice Project Rule of Law Index 2020*, p. 7, https://worldjusticeproject.org/sites/default/files/documents/WJP-ROLI-2020-Online_0.pdf (accessed 22 Aug. 2020).

[4] World Bank Group, *Doing Business 2020: New Zealand*, p. 4, https://www.doingbusiness.org/content/dam/doingBusiness/country/n/new-zealand/NZL.pdf (accessed 22 Aug. 2020).

1.4 Economy

[11] Gross domestic product (GDP) growth for the year ended December 2019 was 2.3%, and the size of New Zealand's economy in current prices was NZD311 bn. While annual growth in GDP has been slowing from a peak of 3.9% in 2016, growth has still been robust in recent years. As it has elsewhere, the COVID-19 pandemic has markedly altered the outlook for New Zealand. In the first quarter reported that reflected COVID-19's impact, GDP recorded its largest quarterly drop in twenty-nine years. Benefiting from low Government debt levels, the Government's economic response to the COVID-19 pandemic has initially focused on support for individuals, through the wage subsidy scheme, as well as investing in 'shovel ready' infrastructure projects.

[12] Mergers and acquisitions activity, like broader economic activity, has been strong in recent years, though it is facing headwinds in 2020. In general, such activity is dominated by private transactions and overall, transactions are evenly split between purely domestic and international involvement, with focuses on the financial services, technology, agri-business and healthcare sectors. However, takeover activity has been strong in recent years, with a number of significant New Zealand listed companies being taken private.

1.5 Trade and Overseas Investment

[13] With a trade-dependent economy operating at a distance from its export markets, New Zealand is a strong supporter of free and open trade. Over the past thirty years New Zealand's economy has gone from being one of the most regulated in the OECD to one of the least regulated, most free-market based economies.[5] Exports sit around 28% of GDP,[6] and the country actively promotes free trade through international bodies such as the World Trade Organisation, Asia-Pacific Economic Co-operation, and the Association of Southeast Asian Nations (ASEAN).

[14] New Zealand has strong trading relationships in its region including Free Trade Agreements with fifteen Asia-Pacific countries which provide access to over two billion consumers. The country's trading relationship with its nearest neighbour, Australia, is built on the NZ-Australia Closer Economic Relations agreement, considered to be one of the most comprehensive bilateral free trade agreement in the world.

[15] In recent years New Zealand has also entered into a number of significant multilateral agreements, including a free trade agreement encompassing ASEAN, Australia and New Zealand, as well the Comprehensive and Progressive Agreement

[5] New Zealand Immigration, *New Zealand Now, Economic Overview*, https://www.newzealandnow.govt.nz/investing-in-nz/economic-overview (accessed 22 Aug. 2020).

[6] World Integrated Trade Solution, *New Zealand Trade Statistics: Exports, Imports, Products, Tariffs, GDP and Related Development Indicator*, https://wits.worldbank.org/CountryProfile/en/NZL (accessed 22 Aug. 2020). Subject to World Trade Organisation copyright.

for Trans-Pacific Partnership (CPTPP). The CPTPP involves eleven other counties including Australia, Brunei, Canada, Chile, Japan, Malaysia and Mexico, and when it was signed at the end of 2018, the combined economies of these countries contributed 13.3% to world GDP.[7]

[16] Significant investments in New Zealand by overseas persons are regulated by the Overseas Investment Act 2005 (the *Overseas Investment Act*). Consent of the Overseas Investment Office (OIO) is required for overseas investments in significant business assets, sensitive land and transactions in the national interest. While the national interest test had been under consideration for some time, this was introduced under urgency in June 2020 as part of the Government's response to the COVID-19 pandemic with a temporary mandatory notification regime in place for overseas investment in New Zealand. Other reforms aimed to facilitate investment that is beneficial to New Zealand and strengthen other aspects of the regime in order to appropriately manage risks are also expected to be introduced in the near future.

1.6 Main Industries

[17] Favourable natural conditions and sophisticated farming technology support New Zealand's strong primary sector,[8] which includes dairy, sheep, horticulture, winemaking, forestry and fisheries industries.

[18] New Zealand has large manufacturing and service sectors as well as an emerging high-tech sector. The New Zealand film industry has also played an important role. Tourism, an important sector of the national economy, was New Zealand's largest export industry in terms of foreign exchange earnings, for the year ended March 2019 – directly employing 8.4% of the New Zealand workforce.[9] The closure of New Zealand's borders to all but New Zealand citizens throughout much of 2020 in response to the COVID-19 pandemic has been felt heavily by the Tourism industry.

1.7 Culture

[19] New Zealand has a de-regulated and decentralised economy that is open to international competition and is consistently named one of the easiest countries in the world to do business in (ranked first by the World Bank Group in its 'Doing

[7] New Zealand Foreign Affairs & Trade, *Comprehensive and Progressive Agreement for Trans-Pacific Partnership overview*, https://www.mfat.govt.nz/en/trade/free-trade-agreements/free-trade-agreements-in-force/cptpp/cptpp-overview/ (accessed 22 Aug. 2020).

[8] New Zealand Immigration, *New Zealand Now, Economic Overview*, https://www.newzealandnow.govt.nz/investing-in-nz/economic-overview (accessed 22 Aug. 2020).

[9] Tourism New Zealand, *About the Tourism Industry*, https://www.tourismnewzealand.com/about/about-the-tourism-industy/ (accessed 22 Aug. 2020).

Business 2020' report and regularly featured as one of the least corrupt counties in the world by Transparency International).

[20] New Zealand has a highly informal and relaxed culture reflecting its rich and diverse blend of cultures. New Zealanders are generally polite, conflict-averse and relatively indirect communicators; however, intention and meaning in language are usually evident.[10] Equality, fairness and honesty are widely held values in New Zealand and many New Zealanders, both Māori and non-Māori, place a high value on honouring the Treaty. New Zealand has a fast-growing Māori economy which holds NZD50 bn of assets. Concepts based on a Māori world view such as Kaitiakitanga (guardianship and protection), which can often be used to describe a way of managing the environment, are increasingly woven through the wider business sector.

[21] There is also a strong commitment to sustainability in New Zealand. The country has a formal goal of net zero carbon emissions by 2050 and a high proportion of renewable energy with an aim of achieving 100% renewable energy by 2035.[11]

2 REGULATORY FRAMEWORK

2.1 Outline of Corporate and Securities Law

[22] The Companies Act 1993 (the *Companies Act*) is central to corporate regulation in New Zealand and covers not just the laws for companies, shareholders and their directors but also restructuring and insolvency rules.

[23] Following major reform to enable New Zealand's securities law to keep pace with investor and business expectations, the Financial Markets Conduct Act 2013 (the *Financial Markets Conduct Act*) was introduced on 1 December 2014. It is the principal legislation regulating New Zealand's capital markets and financial services.

2.2 Overview of Laws Affecting M&A

2.2.1 Overview of Private M&A

[24] Private M&A is implemented in New Zealand through negotiated sale and purchase agreements, and contractual law is relevant to the terms that are agreed

10 *Evason, Nina. (2016). New Zealand Culture.* Retrieved from, https://culturalatlas.sbs.com.au/new-zealand-culture.

11 National Statement from New Zealand to 23rd Conference of the Parties to the UNFCCC (17 Nov. 2017), https://www.beehive.govt.nz/speech/national-statement-new-zealand-23rd-conference-parties-unfccc (accessed 22 Aug. 2020).

between the parties and the interpretation of those terms. As New Zealand is a common law jurisdiction, a mixture of legislation and case law is relevant to resolving private M&A disputes. Where the terms of a sale and purchase agreement are negotiated between sophisticated commercial parties, judges are likely to uphold those commercial terms and give effect to the commercial intention of the parties.

[25] When implementing a private M&A transaction, parties will need to consider whether any regulatory consents are needed. This will principally involve an analysis of whether consents under the Overseas Investment Act and the Commerce Act 1986 (the *Commerce Act*) will be required. As set out in section 9 of this chapter, specific legislation may also be relevant to the particular industry in which the business being acquired is involved.

[26] The parties will need to consider as part of their due diligence whether specific legal issues arise in connection with the business being acquired, such as employment, property, environmental and intellectual property (IP). From a structuring perspective, the Companies Act (or other legislation applicable to the business vehicle being used to make the acquisition) and tax legislation will also need to be considered.

[27] It must be remembered that the Takeovers Code in New Zealand (the *Takeovers Code*) applies to more than just listed companies. The definition of 'Code companies' includes:

- entities which have been listed on a licensed market in the last twelve months (but are no longer listed); or
- which have fifty or more shareholders (with voting rights) and fifty or more share parcels and meet certain financial thresholds.

[28] A scheme of arrangement under the Companies Act can be used for much wider purposes than implementing a takeover of a Code company. Under a scheme of arrangement, the High Court has the power to approve a wide range of corporate restructurings or reorganisations of the share capital of a company (including share transfers, cancellations, issues of shares and amalgamations of companies) and make these binding on the company and any other person the court thinks fit (including shareholders and creditors).

2.2.2 Overview of Public M&A

[29] The acquisition of a listed company must either be undertaken by a takeover offer which complies with the requirements of the Takeovers Code or by way of a scheme of arrangement. In terms of oversight, transactions under the Takeovers Code are regulated by the Takeovers Panel and a scheme of arrangement must also be approved by the courts and shareholders.

[30] Further information on takeovers and schemes of arrangement is set out in section 6 of this chapter.

[31] The Financial Markets Conduct Act and the Financial Markets Conduct Regulations 2014 (the *Financial Markets Conduct Regulations*) may also be relevant to some sales of financial products.

2.3 Relevant Regulatory Authorities

2.3.1 Overseas Investment Office

[32] The OIO is responsible for approving applications by overseas persons to invest in New Zealand. The Overseas Investment Act and the Overseas Investment Regulations confer a broad discretion on the OIO to grant consent, with or without conditions or to refuse consent to an application. The OIO operates under the Minister of Finance, and for applications involving sensitive land and fisheries, the Minister of Land Information and the Minister of Fisheries, respectively are also responsible.

[33] *See* section 7 of this chapter for further information on OIO considerations in New Zealand M&A transactions.

2.3.2 Commerce Commission

[34] The New Zealand Commerce Commission (the *Commission*) is the regulatory body that oversees the enforcement of New Zealand's laws relating to:

- competition or anti-trust (under the Commerce Act);
- economic regulation of monopolies in certain industries such as electricity, gas, telecommunications, dairy and the airport sector (under the Commerce Act);
- fair trading (under the Fair Trading Act 1986); and
- consumer credit contracts (under the Credit Contracts and Consumer Finance Act 2003).

See section 8 of this chapter for further information on competition considerations in New Zealand M&A transactions.

2.3.3 Financial Markets Authority

[35] The Financial Markets Authority (FMA) is the New Zealand government agency responsible for enforcing securities, financial reporting and company law as they apply to financial services and securities markets. The FMA regulates fund-raising activity in New Zealand, which is governed by the Financial Markets Conduct Act and accompanying Financial Markets Conduct Regulations. The FMA's regulatory functions and powers include monitoring and supervision, investigation and enforcement, policy and guidance and licensing of financial markets participants.

[36] *See* section 4.2 of this chapter for further information on FMA considerations in New Zealand M&A transactions.

2.3.4 NZX

[37] NZX Limited (NZX) operates and regulates New Zealand's licensed securities trading exchanges. NZX itself is a publicly held New Zealand company, listed on its main board stock exchange.

[38] NZX regulates its securities markets by way of the NZX Listing Rules and is a co-regulator under the Financial Markets Conduct Act in relation to continuous disclosure, market manipulation and insider trading. NZX's key regulatory functions are performed by NZX Regulation (a separate function within NZX).

[39] As both the operator and regulator of its licensed securities markets, NZX is subject to a regulatory framework under the Financial Markets Conduct Act which provides for regulation by FMA of both the markets NZX operates and NZX itself as a licensed market operator.

[40] *See* section 4.3 of this chapter for further information on NZX considerations in New Zealand M&A transactions.

2.4 Business Vehicles

[41] New Zealand has a full range of different types of business vehicles. Specific advice should be sought on the most appropriate form for each investment in New Zealand, taking into account the particular facts, nature of the business and investment and tax considerations.

2.4.1 Limited Liability Company

[42] The most common business vehicle in New Zealand is a company limited by shares. New Zealand no longer distinguishes between public and private limited liability companies, although if a company is listed on the New Zealand Stock Exchange additional requirements will apply to it through the Financial Markets Conduct Act and NZX Listing Rules.

[43] Unless the constitution of a limited liability company specifies otherwise, the liability of each shareholder is limited to the amount of share capital that shareholder has agreed to acquire or be issued. When a shareholder has paid all of the money payable on its shares, that shareholder has no additional liability to contribute to the capital of the company.

[44] It is possible for a company to be incorporated with unlimited liability or limited by guarantee; however, these types of companies are rare.

[45] Further information on the laws applying to companies is included in section 3 of this chapter.

2.4.2 Overseas Branch

[46] Where a company incorporated outside of New Zealand wishes to carry on business in New Zealand but it is not incorporated in New Zealand, that overseas company must register a branch in New Zealand within ten working days of commencement of carrying on business in New Zealand.

[47] The Companies Act does not exhaustively define what constitutes an overseas company carrying on business in New Zealand. Instead, the Companies Act notes that this includes administering, managing or dealing with property in New Zealand as an agent, personal representative or trustee (and whether though an agent or in any other manner). It also includes establishing or using a share transfer office or a share registration office in New Zealand. However, the Companies Act confirms that an overseas company does not carry on business in New Zealand merely because it maintains a bank account in New Zealand, conducts an isolated transaction that is completed within thirty-one days (and not one of a similar type of transactions repeated from time to time), solicits or procures business that becomes a binding contract only if the order is accepted outside New Zealand or it invests in funds or holds a property in New Zealand.

[48] An overseas branch is subject to continuing statutory reporting obligations prescribed by the Companies Act, including filing audited financial statements if it is a 'large' company[12] and an annual return with the Companies Office.

[49] *See* section 3.2 of this chapter for more information in relation to annual filing and reporting requirements.

2.4.3 Co-operative Companies

[50] There are also a number of 'co-operative companies' in New Zealand, which reflect the country's strong history of primary production. A 'co-operative company' must have as its principal activity a 'co-operative activity' (and state that in its constitution) and not less than 60% of the voting rights must be held by its transacting shareholders.

[51] 'Co-operative activity' means one or more prescribed matters such as:

- supplying or providing shareholders with goods or services;
- processing or marketing goods or services supplied or provided by its shareholders; and
- entering into any other commercial transactions with the shareholders of the company.

[52] Co-operative companies are regulated by the Co-operative Companies Act 1996 and certain provisions of the Companies Act also apply to them.

[12] Pursuant to s. 45(2) of the Financial Reporting Act 2013, an overseas company or an overseas branch is considered 'large' if as at the balance date of each of the two preceding accounting periods: (a) total assets of the entity and its subsidiaries (if any) exceed NZD20 m; or (b) total revenue of the entity and its subsidiaries (if any) exceeds NZD10 m.

2.4.4 Partnerships

[53] Partnerships in New Zealand can either be a partnership, regulated under the Partnership Act 1908 (the *Partnership Act*), or a limited partnership, regulated under the Limited Partnership Act 2008 (the *Limited Partnership Act*).

Partnership

[54] A partnership is not a separate legal entity; each partner is jointly and severally liable for the liabilities of the partnership and has the ability, in carrying on the business of the partnership, to bind the partnership and other partners. A partnership will usually have a comprehensive partnership agreement in place, which can modify or avoid certain provisions of the Partnership Act that would otherwise apply.

Limited Partnership

[55] By contrast, limited partnerships are separate legal entities and are registered on the Limited Partnerships Register.

[56] All limited partnerships must have a written partnership agreement that governs the terms and conditions of the partnership relationship and at least one general partner and one limited partner (and the same person cannot be both the general partner and a limited partner).

[57] Each type of partner incurs different liability risks. General partners are involved with the carrying on of the business and can be liable for the liabilities of the partnership to the extent that these cannot be paid by the limited partnership itself. Limited partners must not take part in the management of the limited partnership and, provided that they do not do so, are only liable proportionately to the capital they have contributed to the partnership and are not liable for the debts and liabilities of the limited partnership itself.

2.4.5 Joint Venture

[58] Joint ventures typically take the form of an incorporated vehicle, most commonly a limited liability company. A joint venture agreement or shareholders' agreement will set out the particular rights and obligations of the shareholders and the company, including provisions relating to how significant decisions and business plans for the joint venture will be made, whether by directors or shareholders, how capital will be contributed and how a sale of shares or the joint venture will be conducted. A constitution will also typically be adopted for the incorporated company, although this focuses more on the corporate rights and obligations, such as director appointment, shareholder meetings and rights on a sale of shares, rather than the commercial terms.

[59] Unincorporated joint ventures are also possible by the parties agreeing to the commercial terms of the arrangement through a joint venture agreement alone.

3 COMPANY LAW

3.1 Incorporation of a Company

3.1.1 Overview of Process

[60] A company is incorporated once the application is accepted by the Registrar of Companies. The application process is facilitated online by the New Zealand Companies Office (the *Companies Office*) and is governed by the Companies Act. Provided all information required to support the application has been collated, the company can be incorporated within one to two days of the application being submitted (depending on whether the Companies Office requires further information to support the application).

[61] To be incorporated, a company must have:

- the company name (which must have already been reserved);
- at least one shareholder;
- at least one share which will be issued upon incorporation;
- at least one director (*see* section 3.3 of this chapter for information on director eligibility requirements in New Zealand);
- the prescribed information in relation to each shareholder and director (the requirements vary depending on whether that shareholder or director is a resident in New Zealand or not and can include identity verification requirements);
- completed shareholder and director consent forms; and
- a copy of the company's constitution, if it wishes to adopt one on incorporation.

[62] Once the application is accepted and the company is incorporated, the company will be issued a certificate of incorporation electronically and will be able to start trading immediately.

[63] New Zealand only has one type of company, and the Companies Act does not distinguish between private and public companies.

3.1.2 Company Constitution

[64] A company's constitution sets out the powers, rights and obligations of the shareholders, board and the company itself. It is binding between the company and its shareholders as well as between each of the shareholders in accordance with its terms.

[65] A company is not required to adopt a constitution. Where a company does not adopt a constitution, the company, the board, each director and each shareholder will have the rights, powers, duties, and obligations set out in the Companies Act.

[66] However, the Companies Act permits a company to modify and simplify some corporate governance matters if those matters are permitted by the company's constitution. As examples, a constitution can include pre-emptive rights on the transfer of shares, permit the company to issue shares other than pro-rata to its shareholders, permit the issue of shares instead of dividends and permit the company to buy-back its own shares. For these reasons, many New Zealand companies do adopt a constitution.

[67] A company may adopt a constitution at incorporation or at any point after incorporation, by passing a special resolution of its shareholders. A special resolution requires a majority of 75% of the votes of shareholders entitled to vote and voting on the resolution. The constitution can be amended or revoked by the same method. If a shareholder votes against such resolution, minority buy-out rights will apply (*see* section 3.4.4 of this chapter).

[68] Once adopted, the constitution must be filed with the Companies Office and will be publicly available.

3.2 Financial Reporting and Other Annual Obligations

3.2.1 Annual Return

[69] An annual return must be filed each year (except the year of incorporation) by every company and limited partnership. An annual return confirms the accuracy, or updates, publicly available information about a company or limited partnership and is a prescribed form provided by the Companies Office.

3.2.2 Financial Statements

[70] While all companies are required to keep accounting records that correctly record the transactions of the company, only certain companies need to comply with the financial reporting requirements under the Companies Act. A company is required to prepare audited financial or group financial statements within five[13] months of their balance date if they are:

- a 'large' company;[14]
- a publicly listed entity;
- a large overseas company;
- any company with ten or more shareholders unless the company has opted out of compliance (which requires a shareholders' resolution to be passed by

[13] Listed companies need to prepare their audited financial statements in a shorter time frame under the NZX Listing Rules.

[14] A 'large' company is an active entity for whom either (a) at the balance date of each of the two preceding accounting periods, the total assets of the entity and its subsidiaries (if any) exceed NZD60 m; or (b) in each of the two preceding accounting periods, the total revenue of the entity and its subsidiaries (if any) exceeds NZD30 m.

at least 95% of shareholders who are entitled to vote and voting on the matter); or

- every other company with fewer than ten shareholders if the company has opted into compliance (which requires a shareholders' resolution to be passed by at least 95% of shareholders who are entitled to vote and voting on the matter).

[71] Where a company is required to prepare financial or group financial statements, those statements must be filed with the Companies Office.

3.2.3 Annual Reports

[72] Certain companies must also prepare an annual report on the affairs of the company, and send these to shareholders, within five months after the balance date of the company but before the date fixed for the annual meeting of shareholders.

[73] A company is required to prepare an annual report if it is:

- a 'large' company[15] unless shareholders holding at least 95% of the voting shares of the company agree that an annual report need not be prepared;
- a publicly listed entity;
- any company with ten or more shareholders unless the company has opted out of compliance (which requires a shareholders' resolution to be passed by at least 95% of shareholders who are entitled to vote and voting on the matter); or
- every other company with fewer than ten shareholders if the company has opted into compliance (which requires a shareholders' resolution to be passed by at least 95% of shareholders who are entitled to vote and voting on the matter).

[74] The annual report must include copies of the financial statements and any auditor's report required as well as other prescribed information about the company, including a description of, as far as the board considers material and not harmful to the business, any change during the accounting period in the nature of the business.

3.3 Directors

3.3.1 New Zealand Requirements

[75] The Companies Act and a company's constitution govern the appointment, removal and eligibility of directors of a company.

[15] A 'large' company is an active entity for whom either (a) at the balance date of each of the two preceding accounting periods, the total assets of the entity and its subsidiaries (if any) exceed NZD60 m; or (b) in each of the two preceding accounting periods, the total revenue of the entity and its subsidiaries (if any) exceed NZD30 m.

[76] Every company must have one or more directors and at least one of those directors must either live in:

- New Zealand; or
- Australia, and be a director of a company incorporated in Australia.

[77] In addition, every director must meet the eligibility requirements to be a director. In summary, a person may be disqualified from being appointed as a director of a company if that person is:

- under 18 years of age;
- an undischarged bankrupt; and/or
- prohibited from being a director by the Companies Act or the Insolvency Act 2006.

[78] These requirements also incorporate any person who has been prohibited from being a director, general partner or promoter of, or taking part in the management of, an overseas company or overseas limited partnership under overseas law.

3.3.2 Appointment and Removal

Appointment

[79] Provided a person is not disqualified from being appointed as a director, a person may be appointed on incorporation or at any time after by way of an ordinary resolution of the company. An ordinary resolution may be passed by a simple majority of votes of those shareholders entitled to vote and voting on the resolution. The Companies Act also permits the constitution to specify other methods of appointment of directors, such as a written notice of the sole shareholder.

Resignation

[80] A director may resign by signing a written notice of resignation and delivering it to the address for service of the company. This notice of resignation is effective from when it is received at that address or at a later time specified in the notice.

[81] A director will also cease to hold office if they become disqualified because they no longer meet the eligibility criteria or die.

Removal

[82] Subject to any other methods being specified in the constitution of a company, the shareholders may remove a director of the company by way of ordinary resolution passed at a meeting called for the purpose of removing that director.

3.3.3 Directors' Duties

[83] The Companies Act codifies a number of duties of directors which arose at common law. This section of this chapter summarises the key directors' duties that are relevant in an M&A context, being the:

- duty to act in good faith and in best interests of the company;
- requirement for powers to be exercised for proper purpose;
- duty not to incur obligations the company cannot meet; and
- duty of care owed by directors.

[84] In addition to these duties, directors must also comply with the Companies Act and constitution and not engage in reckless trading.

Duty to Act in Best Interests

[85] The Companies Act requires that a director acts in good faith and in what the director believes to be in the best interests of the company. That is, the director must not put their own interests or the interests of others ahead of the interests of the company.

[86] Unlike many jurisdictions, the Companies Act does permit a director to act in the best interests of the company's holding company, rather than the best interests of the company. However, a director may only do so if this is expressly permitted in the constitution of the company and, if the company is not a wholly owned subsidiary, all of the shareholders have agreed.

[87] The interests of other stakeholders, such as employees, suppliers, customers or the environment, do not expressly have to be taken into account under the Companies Act, although if the company is nearing insolvency, the interests of creditors do need to be taken into account.

Duty to Exercise Powers for Proper Purpose

[88] A director must exercise its power for a proper purpose and not abuse their position to act for improper reasons. While this appears to be a similar duty to the duty to act in the best interests of the company, a director can be acting in the best interests of the company and yet still be found to have exercised their powers for an improper purpose.

Duty Not to Incur Obligations the Company Cannot Meet

[89] A director of a company must not agree to the company incurring an obligation unless the director believes at that time, on reasonable grounds, that the company will be able to perform the obligation when it is required to do so.

[90] In order to satisfy this duty, the director's belief must be based on reasonable grounds. This means that the director must have sufficient knowledge of the company's position and its ability to be able to meet its obligations. Claiming ignorance on these matters will not be a defence as it is implicit in the duty that the director must take sufficient steps to obtain the necessary knowledge.

Duty of Care

[91] A director must exercise the care, diligence and skill that a reasonable director would exercise in the same circumstances taking into account (but without limitation):

- the nature of the company;
- the nature of the decisions; and
- the position of the director and the nature of the responsibilities undertaken by him or her.

[92] While the Companies Act gives some recognition to the fact that different directors will have different skill sets and responsibilities, the duty still requires all directors to exercise the objective standard of the reasonable director and so a director may not absolve themselves purely because they personally did not know something or ask sufficient questions.

[93] The Companies Act does, however, recognise that directors may rely on information prepared by management or professional advisers, provided there are reasonable grounds to believe that such person is reasonably competent in that area. The director still needs to make proper inquiry to confirm if their reliance on this information is warranted.

3.3.4 Interested Directors

[94] All directors must promptly disclose any interests in a transaction or proposed transaction with the company. There are limited exceptions to this rule, including if the transaction is to be entered into in the ordinary course of business and on usual terms and conditions. A transaction entered into by a company in which a director is interested can be avoided by the company within three months after the shareholders receive notice of it, unless the company receives fair value. However, this will not affect the title or interest of a person in or to property which that person has acquired from a person other than the company, for valuable consideration and without knowledge of the circumstances.

[95] Subject to the contrary being included in the constitution of a company, the Companies Act permits an interested director to vote on, attend board meetings in respect of and do any other things in his or her capacity as a director in relation to that transaction as if the director were not interested in it.

3.3.5 Role of Management

[96] The business and affairs of the company are to be managed by, or under the direction or supervision of, the board of directors. In practice, day-to-day management decisions are often delegated to a specific management team. However, the Companies Act prohibits the board from delegating certain decisions, such as approving a distribution, giving financial assistance or approving the transfer of shares. The constitution may also limit other matters which the board may not delegate.

[97] Where a power is delegated, the board still remains responsible for the exercise of that power, unless the board believed on reasonable grounds that the person to whom the power was delegated would exercise power in accordance with the Companies Act and constitution, and the board monitored the exercise of the power using reasonable methods.

[98] There is no requirement for a member of management to be a director of a company.

3.4 Shareholder Approvals

3.4.1 Overview

[99] The Companies Act requires certain matters to receive the approval of shareholders before a company can undertake them. There are three key categories where shareholder approvals are required, being matters requiring:

(1) approval by ordinary resolution;
(2) approval by special resolution; and
(3) the consent of all entitled persons.

[100] A shareholder resolution can either be passed at a meeting of the company or by way of written resolution.

3.4.2 Ordinary Resolution

[101] Unless the Companies Act specifies that a special resolution is required (*see* below) or the constitution otherwise requires, a power reserved to shareholders by the Companies Act must be passed by ordinary resolution. An ordinary resolution is passed if a simple majority of the votes of the shareholders of the company, who are entitled to vote and are voting on the resolution, are in favour of the matter.

3.4.3 Special Resolution

[102] A special resolution requires the approval of 75% of the votes of the shareholders of the company who are entitled to vote and are voting on the resolution (or, if a higher majority is required by the constitution, that higher majority).

[103] The Companies Act requires the following matters be approved by a special resolution:

- the adoption, alteration or revocation of a constitution;
- a 'major transaction';
- an amalgamation; and
- the commencement of a liquidation of a company.

[104] In addition, the alteration of any rights of an interest group of shareholders will require a special resolution of that interest group before it can be implemented.

[105] In the context of an M&A transaction, the need for shareholder approvals of 'major transactions' can be of particular relevance. A 'major transaction' is:

- the acquisition of assets, the value of which is more than half the value of the company's assets before the acquisition;
- the disposal of assets of the company, the value of which is more than half the value of the company's assets before the disposition; or
- a transaction that has, or is likely to have, the effect of the company acquiring rights or interests or incurring obligations or liabilities, including contingent liabilities, the value of which is more than half the value of the company's assets before the transaction.

[106] The seller will need to consider whether the sale is sufficiently large, or the terms of the sale agreement give rise to sufficient liabilities, to meet these thresholds. Separately the purchaser will need to consider whether any actions it is taking in connection with the sale constitute a major transaction, particularly if the entity which is the purchaser is a special purpose vehicle incorporated for the purposes of the transaction which has no other assets.

3.4.4 Minority Buy-Out Rights

[107] The Companies Act grants buy-out rights to minority shareholders who vote against certain significant transactions in order to prevent minority shareholders from being forced to continue to hold shares in the company if they disagree with those particular matters.

[108] Minority buy-out rights apply if the shareholders approve by special resolution:

- the adoption, alteration or revocation of a constitution;
- a 'major transaction';
- an amalgamation; or
- the taking of an action which affects the rights of an interest group of shareholders, but the minority shareholders vote all of their shares against the resolution to approve such matter.

[109] In such a scenario, the minority shareholder may give notice that he or she wishes to exercise his or her minority buy-out rights within ten business days of the relevant resolution being passed. The minority shareholder then has the right to have his or her shares valued and require the company, or some other person determined by the board, to purchase his or her shares at that price. The buy-out price must be a fair and reasonable price for those shares, and if the minority shareholder objects to the price determined by the board, the price will be determined by arbitration.

[110] However, there are limited circumstances where a company does not have to comply with the minority buy-out rights, including if:

- the purchase would be disproportionately damaging to the company;
- the company cannot reasonably be required to finance the purchase;
- it would not be just and equitable to require the company to purchase the shares;
- if the company is insolvent; or
- the resolution giving rise to the minority buy-out rights is rescinded by way of special resolution.

3.4.5 Entitled Persons Process

[111] The Companies Act permits the company to undertake certain transactions without following the procedure for that transaction set out in the Companies Act if all entitled persons have agreed in writing. An 'entitled person' is a shareholder or a person upon whom the constitution confers any of the rights and powers of a shareholder.

[112] Matters which can be approved with entitled persons' consent include:

- authorising a dividend;
- approving a discount scheme for shareholders to purchase goods or services sold by the company;
- the acquisition or redemption by the company of its own shares;
- providing financial assistance for the purchase of its shares;
- authorising any payment of remuneration, benefits, compensation for loss of office, loans and guarantees in relation to directors;
- entering into a transaction in which a director is interested; and
- issuing shares.

[113] For all of the above matters, other than the issuance of shares, in addition to obtaining the consent of all entitled persons, the board must also be satisfied on reasonable grounds that the company will, immediately after the exercise of the power, satisfy the solvency test. The solvency test broadly requires that the company must be able to pay its debts as they become due and that the value of the company's assets must be greater than the value of its liabilities, including contingent liabilities.

3.5 Shares

3.5.1 Transfer of Shares

[114] Shares are generally able to be easily transferred under New Zealand law, by the signing of a share transfer form and the registration of the new shareholder in the company's share register. However, the constitution of a company may set out additional processes which need to be followed in order to transfer shares, such as pre-emptive rights, rights of first refusal and tag and drag-along provisions.

[115] The share register is the prime facie evidence of legal title to the shares. Most shares in New Zealand do not have share certificates, and so it is important that the purchaser requires the share register to be updated by the company to reflect its ownership.

3.5.2 Issuing Shares

[116] The Companies Act provides a number of methods for a company to issue shares.

[117] Generally, the board of the company may issue shares at any time and in any number that the board thinks fit. The constitution may also provide additional methods for issuing shares; however, notwithstanding any limitation in the company's constitution, the board can issue shares with the approval of shareholders by special resolution and, if applicable, the approval of any interest groups. Shares can also be issued with the consent of all entitled persons.

[118] Under the Companies Act, existing shareholders have pre-emptive rights to be issued shares on a pro-rata basis unless the constitution provides otherwise.

[119] The board is responsible for determining the consideration for the shares and the terms of issue, both of which must be fair and reasonable to the company and to all existing shareholders. The consideration for shares may take any form, including future services to the company, but shares are predominately issued for cash. If shares are to be issued for non-cash consideration, the board must determine the reasonable present cash value of the consideration and determine that this is not less than the amount to be credited for the issue of shares. However, if the consent of entitled persons is obtained, the board can issue shares other than in accordance with these requirements.

[120] A share is deemed to be issued when it is entered on the company's share register. As with the transfer of shares, it is important that the share register is kept up to date with what shares have been issued, and to whom. Notice must also be given to the Companies Office within ten business days of the issue of shares.

3.5.3 Buy-Backs

[121] A company may only buy-back its own shares if it is permitted to do so under its constitution and:

- the offer is to all shareholders on a pro-rata basis;
- the offer is to one or more shareholders and either all shareholders consent in writing to the buy-back or the disclosure process under the Companies Act (and if the company is listed, the NZX Listing Rules) is followed; or
- the company obtains the consent of all entitled persons to provide such financial assistance.

[122] Under the first two options above, the board must determine that the buy-back is in the best interests of the company, the terms of the offer and the consideration are fair and reasonable to the company and it is not aware of any non-public material information which would make the terms of the offer and consideration offered unfair to the shareholders accepting the offer.

3.5.4 Redemption of Shares

[123] Shares are only redeemable if the constitution permits the redemption of shares and the constitution or terms of issue of those shares provide for the redemption of those shares. Shares can either be redeemed at the option of the shareholder, the option of the company or on a fixed date.

[124] Like with the buy-back of shares, the company has the option of redeeming shares on a pro-rata basis or through selective redemption, provided the disclosure process in the Companies Act is followed and additional board approvals are obtained. The company must also satisfy the solvency test immediately after the redemption, if the company is electing to redeem shares.

3.5.5 Financial Assistance

[125] Under the Companies Act, a company may provide financial assistance in connection with the purchase of shares issued or to be issued by the company, or by its holding company, if:

- the company obtains the unanimous consent of its shareholder(s) to provide such assistance;
- the board approves such financial assistance on the basis it is of benefit to, and the terms and conditions of it are fair and reasonable to, the shareholders not receiving the assistance and certain disclosures to other shareholders are made;
- the financial assistance does not exceed 5% of shareholder equity and the company must receive fair value for such assistance; or
- the company obtains the consent of all entitled persons to provide such financial assistance.

[126] In each case, the directors voting in favour of giving the financial assistance must sign a certificate confirming that the company will, among other things, satisfy the solvency test immediately after the financial assistance is given.

3.5.6 Dividends and Distributions

[127] A distribution by a company to a shareholder is defined under the Companies Act as:

- the direct or indirect transfer of money or property, other than the company's own shares, to or for the benefit of a shareholder; or
- the incurring of a debt to or for the benefit of a shareholder, in relation to shares held by that shareholder.

[128] The Companies Act provides that the board may authorise a distribution provided that the board is satisfied on reasonable grounds that the company will satisfy the solvency test immediately after the distribution. Generally distributions must be pro-rata to existing shareholders, but the constitution may provide for differential dividends to be paid.

3.5.7 Amalgamations

[129] Two or more companies (other than Code companies) may amalgamate and either continue as one company or become a new company using either the short form or standard procedure in the Companies Act.

[130] A standard amalgamation requires an amalgamation proposal setting out the terms of the amalgamation and any necessary information to be prepared. The amalgamation proposal must be approved by:

- the board of each amalgamating company, confirming that they consider the amalgamation to be in the best interests of the company and that they are satisfied on reasonable grounds that the company will pass a solvency test immediately after amalgamation; and
- the shareholders of each amalgamating company, either by special resolution or, if there are interest groups, by each of those interest groups.

[131] The amalgamation proposal must also be given to each secured creditor and public notice of the proposal must also be given. All approvals and certificates required under the Companies Act must be filed with the Companies Office and the Registrar will then issue a certificate of amalgamation. At this point, all rights and liabilities of the amalgamating companies will be transferred to the amalgamated company.

[132] A short-form amalgamation may be undertaken instead if the companies are related to each other. The board of each amalgamating company must approve the amalgamation, confirming that they consider the amalgamation to be in the best interests of the company and that they are satisfied on reasonable grounds that the company will pass a solvency test immediately after amalgamation. Notice of the proposed amalgamation must also be given to each secured creditor. These approvals and notices must also be filed with the Companies Office in order for the certificate of amalgamation to be issued.

4 SECURITIES LAW AND LISTED COMPANIES

4.1 Overview

[133] Securities law in New Zealand is principally governed by the Financial Markets Conduct Act 2013 (the *Financial Markets Conduct Act*). The Financial Markets

Conduct Act regulates primary and secondary market transactions, including disclosure requirements for offers of securities, insider trading and market manipulation prohibitions, continuous disclosure rules for listed entities and licensing requirements for market participants (among other matters). The Financial Markets Conduct Act is designed to strengthen New Zealand's capital markets and make it easier for businesses to access capital while maintaining a high standard of integrity, which is crucial for business confidence.

[134] The application of these securities laws will be of particular relevance where an M&A transaction involves quoted or unquoted securities in New Zealand either as the asset being acquired or as a component of the consideration.[16]

[135] The Financial Markets Conduct Act uses the term 'financial products' to refer to what would commonly be known in other jurisdictions as 'securities'. Financial products include equity securities, debt securities and managed investment products.

4.2 Financial Markets Conduct Act

4.2.1 Fair Dealing Provisions

[136] The Financial Markets Conduct Act sets out certain behavioural standards for persons who are in trade (i.e., as part of their business, profession or a commercial undertaking), operate in the financial markets or deal in financial products. These are referred to as the 'fair dealing' provisions.

[137] Those 'fair dealing' provisions prohibit:

- misleading or deceptive conduct;
- conduct that is likely to mislead or deceive;
- false or misleading representations;
- unsubstantiated representations; and
- offers of financial products in the course of unsolicited meetings.

[138] These provisions apply to conduct both in and outside New Zealand by any person who is resident, incorporated, registered or carrying on business in New Zealand to the extent that the conduct relates to dealing in financial products that occurs (in part or otherwise) within New Zealand. They also apply to both retail and institutional investors in financial products.

[139] A breach of any of these general fair dealing provisions may give rise to civil liability including:

[16] This chapter does not consider the requirements of the Financial Markets Conduct Act in the context of an issue of new financial products, for which a product disclosure statement (similar to a prospectus), register entry and other regulatory filings may be required unless an exemption is available. Specific advice should be sought in connection with any issue of new financial products, either to institutional or retail investors.

- a pecuniary penalty not exceeding the greater of the consideration for the relevant transaction;
- three times the gain made or loss avoided; and
- NZD1 m in the case of an individual or NZD5 m in any other case.

4.2.2 Insider Trading/Market Manipulation

[140] The regulation of insider trading and market manipulation, and associated sanctions, reflect the view that such misconduct negatively impacts the integrity and reputation of New Zealand's markets, and the confidence of people investing in them.

Insider Trading

[141] Prohibitions on insider trading by 'information insiders' under the Financial Markets Conduct Act apply to quoted financial products only – i.e., securities listed on a stock exchange in New Zealand.

[142] An 'information insider' is a person who:

- has 'material information' relating to a listed issuer that is not generally available to the market;
- knows or ought reasonably to know that the information they possess is material information; and
- knows or ought reasonably to know that the information they possess is not generally available to the market.

[143] Importantly, a listed issuer can be an information insider of itself.

[144] 'Material information' is defined in the Financial Markets Conduct Act, for the purposes of the insider trading provisions, as information that:

- a reasonable person would expect, if it were generally available to the market, to have a material effect on the price of quoted financial products of the listed issuer; and
- relates to particular financial products, a particular listed issuer, or particular listed issuers, rather than to financial products generally or listed issuers generally.

[145] An 'information insider' is prohibited under the Financial Markets Conduct Act from engaging in the following conduct:

- trading in quoted financial products of a listed issuer;
- disclosing (directly or indirectly) inside information to another person that they know (or ought reasonably to know) will, or is likely to, trade financial products of the listed issuer, or advise or encourage another person to trade or hold those products; or
- advising or encouraging (directly or indirectly) another person to trade or hold quoted financial products of a listed issuer.

[146] Breach of the insider trading prohibitions may result in criminal or civil liability.

[147] A number of exceptions to the insider trading prohibition apply, including where required by law (such as minority buy-out rights under the Companies Act), when underwriting a securities offer or in, in certain circumstances, a takeover or scheme of arrangement.

[148] A range of defences is available to insider trading including:

- if the information insider did not know, or could not reasonably be expected to know, of the trading (e.g., if the person jointly owned the shares);
- if the inside information was independently obtained by the person through research or analysis, not from the listed issuer;
- both parties to the trade had the same inside information;
- certain trades in options, undertaken in accordance with a fixed trading plan or where an information barrier applied.

Market Manipulation

[149] The Financial Markets Conduct Act also restricts conduct that amounts to market manipulation. The market manipulation prohibitions in the Financial Markets Conduct Act apply to any quoted financial product.

[150] The market manipulation provisions prohibit matters designed to distort the market for trading in financial products and focus on disseminating false or misleading information and distorting the market for that financial product.

[151] The making of a statement or dissemination of information is prohibited if:

- a material aspect of that statement or information is false or materially misleading; and
- the person knew or ought to have known that a material aspect of that statement or information is false or materially misleading; and
- the statement or information was either likely to induce a person to trade, have the effect of increasing, reducing, maintaining or stabilising the price of that financial product; or induce a person to vote in a particular way (or abstain from voting).

[152] If a person has actual knowledge that the statement or information was false in a material aspect or was materially misleading, criminal and civil liability applies.

[153] An action or omission which will have, or is likely to have, the effect of creating or causing the creation of a false or misleading appearance of active trading or the supply, demand, price or value of those financial products is prohibited if the person knew, or ought reasonably to have known that the person's act or omission would, or was likely to, have that effect.

[154] Again if a person has actual knowledge that the act or omission will have that effect on the market, criminal and civil liability applies.

[155] There are some limited exemptions, such as for conduct regulated by the Takeovers Code and stabilising the market following an initial public offering. It is also a defence if the person can prove that the trading in financial products was made in conformity with accepted market practices and for a proper purpose, although the Financial Markets Conduct Act does not define these matters.

4.2.3 On-Sale of Financial Products

[156] The Financial Markets Conduct Act is primarily focussed on the issue of financial products, and as such, it is uncommon for the Financial Markets Conduct Act's disclosure or registration requirements to apply to a private M&A transaction, absent a unique feature such as shares being issued as consideration for the transaction. However, the Financial Markets Conduct Act does regulate the sale of financial products in a limited number of circumstances.

[157] These circumstances include:

- if the financial products were issued with a view to the original holder dealing in those products, the offer for sale is made within twelve months of the date of issue and no regulated offer of those products has already been made;
- if the issuer is selling unquoted financial products in itself and is also advising, encouraging or knowingly assisting that offer; or
- the party offering the financial products for sale controls the issuer and the financial products are unquoted or are quoted but not offered for sale in the ordinary course of trading on a licensed market.

[158] Where the restrictions on sales of financial products do apply, the usual exemptions (such as for sales to institutional investors) from the preparation of a product disclosure statement (similar to a prospectus in other jurisdictions) and registration of that statement may also be available.

4.3 NZX Listing Rules

4.3.1 Overview

[159] The NZX Listing Rules regulate the conduct, governance, corporate actions and disclosure obligations of issuers listed on the NZX. All NZX listed issuers are required to comply with the NZX Listing Rules and incorporate their provisions into their constitution.

[160] In the context of an M&A transaction, if an entity which is part of a group listed on the NZX is either acquiring or selling an asset, the NZX Listing Rules should be considered as they may require certain approvals or disclosures be made.

4.3.2 Major Transactions

[161] Shareholder approval is required before an issuer can complete any transaction, or series of related transactions, which would involve the acquisition, sale, lease, exchange or other disposal of assets if this would:

- significantly change the nature of the issuer's business (whether directly or indirectly); or
- involve a gross value of greater than 50% of the average market capitalisation of the issuer.

[162] Approval by a simple majority of shareholders entitled to vote and voting on the transaction will be required, unless the transaction is also subject to the major transaction rules in the Companies Act, in which case a special resolution of shareholders will be required. *See* section 3.4(c).

4.3.3 Related Party Transactions

[163] The NZX Listing Rules also require shareholder approval before an issuer can complete a material transaction with a related party. The purpose of the rule is to ensure that shareholders have an opportunity to consider, and vote on, such transactions where there is, or may be a perception of, the potential for undue influence by a related party on an issuer's decision to enter into a transaction or agree to its terms.

[164] A related party is broadly defined and captures:

- directors and senior managers of the issuer;
- shareholders who hold more than 10% of the voting shares of that issuer;
- associated persons of the issuer (broadly speaking a related body corporate, persons acting jointly or in concert or a person who is able exercise a substantial degree of influence over another person); or
- persons who are intended to become a related party.

[165] Material transactions also cover a wide range of potential transactions including:

- acquiring or disposing of assets having an aggregate net value of more than 10% of the issuer's average market capitalisation;
- borrowing or lending money having an aggregate net value of more than 10% of the issuer's average market capitalisation;
- entering into a guarantee, indemnity or similar obligation, or giving security, that could expose an issuer to a liability of more than 10% of the issuer's average market capitalisation; or
- providing or obtaining services where the gross cost to the issuer in any financial year is likely to exceed an amount equal to 1% of the issuer's average market capitalisation.

[166] However, there are a number of exceptions to the related-party rules so that issuers do not have to seek shareholder approval for ordinary course, arm's length, commercial transactions with related parties.

4.3.4 Continuous Disclosure Obligations

[167] A key obligation under the NZX Listing Rules is for an issuer to promptly and without delay disclose material information to the market. Material information has the same meaning given to it as in the Financial Markets Conduct Act.

[168] If an M&A transaction constitutes material information, then an issuer must announce that information. There are certain exceptions to this rule which may apply in the lead up to finalising the terms of the M&A transaction if, for example, the proposal or negotiation of the terms of the transaction is incomplete, the information is confidential and confidentiality is maintained and a reasonable person would not expect the information to be disclosed. Importantly, all three limbs of this test must be met in order to rely on this exception and so if, for example, confidentiality is lost, the issuer must make an announcement even if negotiations are still not complete. Accordingly, the application of these rules should be considered carefully and continuously when an issuer is considering an M&A transaction.

5 PRIVATE M&A

5.1 Asset or Share Sale?

5.1.1 Overview

[169] A fundamental question in any private M&A transaction is whether it will be conducted by way of an asset sale or a share sale. This will result in important differences in the liabilities which a purchaser assumes, due diligence process and terms of the sale agreement.

5.1.2 Asset Sale

[170] An asset sale involves the transfer of individual assets from the purchaser to the seller. Rather than transferring title to the shares, the transaction may involve transferring tangible assets and/or intangible assets. This gives the flexibility for the purchaser to choose which assets of the seller it acquires (and leaves behind), although all of the assets comprising the business are commonly acquired to ensure the business continues as a going concern.

[171] A purchaser will often prefer to acquire assets over shares. This is because an asset sale allows the purchaser to take on the assets of the business without the liabilities, such as tax liabilities, unless it specifically agrees to do so as part of the sale agreement.

[172] The legal process for an asset sale is generally more complicated than that of a share sale. Due diligence will need to focus on the title to, and the process for the transfer of, multiple individual assets. This will often have ramifications in areas such as real property, employment agreements and supply and customer contracts.

The sale agreement will also need to exhaustively list all assets, and any liabilities, being acquired as part of the sale and the mechanism for that transfer, in addition to other usual provisions.

5.1.3 Share Sale

[173] In contrast, a seller will often prefer a share sale to an asset sale. This is not just to ensure a simpler process, and it is also so that the liabilities of the company are sold to the purchaser, subject to any liabilities that the seller contractually agrees to retain (such as tax or environmental indemnities or warranties relating to the state of the business).

[174] Share sales tend to be more common. However, depending on the negotiating strength of the parties, and particularly in a bilateral sales process, an asset sale may be agreed too.

5.2 Due Diligence

[175] Due diligence is an important phase in the sales process and is typically conducted contemporaneously with the negotiation of the sale agreement.

[176] Once appropriate confidentiality arrangements are put in place, access to a virtual data room is granted to the purchaser and their advisors in order to conduct their due diligence investigations. Depending on the size of the deal and nature of the business, a range of different types of due diligence may be conducted, including commercial, legal, financial, tax and sometimes specialist due diligence, such as environmental, IT or insurance.

[177] The scope of due diligence will vary depending on factors such as the purchaser's familiarity with the business or industry, any requirements of any debt financiers and warranty and indemnity insurance. From a legal perspective, the scope tends to focus on what the legal requirements are to implement the transaction (e.g., regulatory approvals or consents of contractual counterparties) and identification of material legal liabilities or non-compliance with laws.

[178] In addition to the data room, purchasers are usually given the opportunity to ask the seller and management of the target business questions to facilitate its understanding of the business, and a management presentation may be made.

[179] Where the seller is undertaking a competitive sales process of a major asset, the seller may conduct vendor due diligence. These reports will give an overview of the business being sold in order for bidders to be able to more quickly understand the issues facing that business and they may also identify issues which the seller wishes to resolve prior to selling the business. However, vendor due diligence is always undertaken from the seller's perspective and will not take into account a purchaser's individual requirements and so should not be relied on as a substitute for the purchaser undertaking its own due diligence.

5.3 Sale Agreement

5.3.1 Overview

[180] The sale agreement will set out the terms on which the shares or assets are to be sold, including how the purchase price will be paid, how the sale will be implemented and any recourse which the purchaser will have against the seller following completion of the sale.

[181] While the Auckland District Law Society maintains a 'standard' form agreement for the sale and purchase of a business, this is typically only used in small scale business transfers. Any other sale is usually undertaken on the terms and conditions of a specifically negotiated sale agreement. As there is a wide variety of terms and conditions which may be agreed, the remaining headings below in this section 5.3 focus on the key terms.

[182] In addition, other transaction documents may be relevant, such as a transitional services agreement in order to assist with the short term provision of shared services to the sold business or a trademark licence agreement for a short term before the sold business is rebranded.

5.3.2 Pre-completion Obligations

[183] Pre-completion obligations tend to fall into three main categories: conditions precedent, restrictions on how the business will be conducted prior to completion and other 'tidy-ups' to occur prior to completion.

[184] Conditions precedent are matters which must, or must not, occur prior to completion; otherwise, a party will have a right to terminate the sale agreement and not complete the transaction. Typically, conditions precedent relate to regulatory approvals which are required at law before the sale can complete. However, other conditions precedent may be negotiated, such as consents required under contracts with a major customer or supplier and no material adverse change occurring between signing and completion.

5.3.3 Consideration Payable

[185] The purchase price for the assets or shares being acquired is usually payable in one lump sum on completion. However, the sale agreement gives broad flexibility for the seller and purchaser to agree with any mechanism they see fit, including requiring a deposit (particularly if OIO or other regulatory approvals are required), purchase price adjustments (either through the preparation of completion statements or locked-box mechanisms), deferred consideration and earn-outs.

5.3.4 Warranties

[186] A warranty is a contractual statement that enables the purchaser to sue for a breach of contract and recover damages in the event that the warranty is untrue, incorrect or misleading. It is uncommon in New Zealand for a breach of a warranty to give rise to a right for a purchaser to terminate the sale agreement.

[187] Limits on recovery, as well as time and financial constraints for making a warranty claim, will also be agreed as part of the sale agreement. Importantly, matters disclosed in writing by the seller to the purchaser (including information in the data room or any disclosure letter) and matters within the purchaser's knowledge, are often excluded from the warranties. Accordingly, if the purchaser obtains a warranty on a certain matter, it is in the seller's interests to disclose any potential problems relating to that matter as part of the purchaser's due diligence.

[188] The range of warranties requested and agreed between the parties will depend on a number of factors, including the nature of the company, business or assets being acquired and the respective bargaining power of the parties. If the transaction involves a sale of shares, the warranties will usually be more extensive because the purchaser is acquiring all of the target company's assets and liabilities, whereas in an asset sale, the purchaser will only take agreed assets and liabilities.

5.3.5 Indemnities

[189] As noted above, a purchaser will be unlikely to have a warranty claim if it has knowledge of an issue. Instead, for issues identified during due diligence, the purchaser will need to seek a specific indemnity for any loss or damage which it suffers as a result of that issue if it is to have recourse.

[190] The most common example is a tax indemnity for any pre-completion taxes which the target company should have paid. Other examples include an environmental indemnity or an indemnity in respect of the target company's obligations under the Holidays Act. *See* sections 11.3, 12.1.3, 14.2.3 and for further information on tax, Holidays Act and environmental indemnities respectively.

5.3.6 Warranty and Indemnity Insurance

[191] Warranty and indemnity insurance is becoming an increasingly common way to cover the risk of a breach of warranties. Commonly, the purchaser will arrange this directly through its broker, although in a competitive process, the seller may undertake the preparatory work and then 'flip' this to the preferred bidder for it to negotiate the final stages directly with the insurer.

[192] A wide range of common warranties and the tax indemnity can usually be covered by the insurance, provided that the purchaser has done sufficient due diligence. There are 'standard' carve-outs for common issues, such as seismic issues, Holidays Act liabilities and transfer pricing. In addition, during the underwriting process, specific exclusions for particular issues may be identified by the insurer. A separate insurance policy may also be needed in order to obtain cover for matters such as environmental or cybersecurity and, if available in the insurance market, cover for new breaches of warranties that arise before signing of the sale agreement but only become known between signing and completion.

5.3.7 Restraints of Trade

[193] While prima facie unenforceable at common law, in the context of a business acquisition a restraint of trade is relatively common, in order to protect the goodwill of the business being purchased.

[194] Restraints can be upheld by the courts if it is reasonable in the interests of the contracting parties and not injurious to the public interest. The courts will consider whether substantive consideration has been provided by the purchaser, the parties are sophisticated, and there is equality of negotiating power, as well as whether the duration, geographical area and scope of activities covered by the restraint are reasonable in the context of the business being acquired. This assessment will be factually specific.

[195] The Commerce Act prohibits agreements that substantially lessen competition or contain a 'cartel' provision. However, limited exceptions to these rules include an exemption for a restraint of trade which is solely for the protection of the purchaser in respect of the goodwill of a business or shares. *See* section 8 for further information on anticompetitive restraints and obtaining clearance from the Commission.

[196] As a general rule, a restraint of trade must not put undue restriction on the ability of the seller, or any other individual subject to the restraint of trade, to earn a livelihood where that person's skills and knowledge are specific to the business that they have just sold or left. Accordingly, restraints of trade which apply to individuals may be less likely to be enforced, than a restraint of trade binding commercial parties. *See* section 12.4 for further information on restraints of trade of employees.

[197] Where a restraint of trade provision is found to be unreasonable, the Contract and Commercial Law Act 2017 (*Contract and Commercial Law Act*) provides a discretion for courts to:

- delete the restraint provision and give effect to the contract as amended;
- modify the restraint provision in order to make it reasonable and give effect to the contract as modified; or
- decline to enforce the contract.

5.3.8 Completion Formalities

[198] *See* sections 12.3, 14.1.4 and 14.3.4 of this chapter for a description of particular formalities for completing the transfer of certain types of assets, including employees, property and IP.

6 TAKEOVERS/SCHEMES OF ARRANGEMENT

6.1 Introduction

[199] The primary methods for taking control of a company to which the Takeovers Code applies are:

- a takeover offer under the Takeovers Code (a *Takeover Offer*); and
- a scheme or arrangement under Part 15 of the Companies Act (a *Scheme*).

[200] This section summarises the primary rules, restrictions and procedures applicable to each method.

6.2 Regulation of Takeovers

6.2.1 Application of the Takeovers Code and the Companies Act

[201] The Takeovers Code is the principal source of regulation of takeovers in New Zealand. The Takeovers Code applies to voting securities in 'Code companies'. 'Code companies' are defined as New Zealand incorporated companies that:

- have, or in the last twelve months have had, financial products that confer voting rights quoted on a licensed market (e.g., equity securities listed on the NZX); or
- have fifty or more shareholders (with voting rights), fifty or more share parcels and meet certain financial thresholds.

[202] As such, the Takeovers Code may apply to the proposed acquisition of an unlisted New Zealand incorporated company that meets the other thresholds.

[203] Schemes are principally governed by Part 15 of the Companies Act. However, the Takeovers Code will also apply to Schemes until the court has made its final order to approve the Scheme.

6.2.2 The Takeovers Panel

[204] The Takeovers Panel (the *Panel*) is responsible for regulating New Zealand's takeovers market and enforcing the Takeovers Code. The Panel is likely to have regular involvement in a takeover of a Code company; from engaging with the parties on Takeovers Code-related issues to reviewing information to be sent to target shareholders.

6.3 The Fundamental Rule

6.3.1 The 'Fundamental Rule'

[205] The fundamental rule of the Takeovers Code is that a party may not become the holder or controller of more than 20% of the voting rights in a Code company, or increase an existing holding of 20% or more of the voting rights in a Code company, other than in compliance with the Takeovers Code.

6.3.2 Exceptions to the Fundamental Rule

[206] The Takeovers Code provides the following methods for a person to hold or control voting rights in a Code company above the fundamental rule thresholds:

- by acquiring voting securities under a full offer or Partial Offer;
- by an acquisition of voting securities that has been approved by an ordinary resolution of the Code company in accordance with the Takeovers Code;
- by an allotment of voting securities in the Code company, approved by an ordinary resolution of the Code company in accordance with the Takeovers Code;
- where the party holds or controls between 50% and 90% of the voting rights in the Code company, by increasing by no more than 5% from the lowest percentage of voting rights held or controlled by that party in the previous twelve months (often referred to as the '5 percent creep rule'); or
- by acquiring voting securities where the person already holds or controls 90% or more of the voting rights in the Code company.

6.3.3 Associates

[207] The scope of the Takeovers Code is extended significantly by the concept of 'associates'. This term is broadly defined and includes persons acting jointly or in concert, persons accustomed to acting in accordance with the wishes of others, related companies, persons with business relationships, personal relationships or other ownership relationships or if the nature of the relationships under the circumstances means that the parties should be regarded as associates.

[208] The Takeovers Code requires that where two or more associates obtain ownership or control of voting rights, the voting rights of those parties must be aggregated for the purpose of complying with the fundamental rule.

[209] It is not a breach of the Takeovers Code for two or more people to be or become associates, even if they together hold or control more than 20% of the voting rights in a Code company. Rather, a breach would arise if one or more parties who are associates and who together hold an excess of 20% of the voting rights in a Code company become the holders or controllers of additional voting rights. At that point the shareholdings of the associates are aggregated for the purpose of determining whether the acquisition complies with the fundamental rule.

6.3.4 Full or Partial Offer

[210] The most commonly used route for increasing a shareholding in a Code company to above 20% of voting securities has been to make a 'full offer' under the Takeovers Code. A full offer is an offer to all shareholders of the Target company on the same terms to purchase all of the equity securities in a Code company.

[211] An offer may also be made under the Takeovers Code for less than all of the voting securities in a Code company (a *Partial Offer*). A Partial Offer must be extended to all holders of voting securities of the Target company.

[212] If there is only one class of voting securities of the target company, a partial takeover offer must be for a specified percentage of the voting securities not held by the offeror (the *Offeror*). If there is more than one class of voting securities, a partial takeover offer must be for the same specified percentage of the voting securities of each class not held by the Offeror. The Offeror must choose a specified percentage that is either:

- a specified percentage that would result in the Offeror holding or controlling more than 50% of the voting securities of the target company (the *Target*); or
- a specified percentage that would result in the Offeror holding or controlling 50% or less, subject to shareholder approval being obtained.

[213] Where an Offeror receives acceptances for more shares than the specified percentage sought, acceptances must be proportionately scaled back.

6.3.5 Shareholder Approval

[214] The Takeovers Code permits voting rights to be increased above the relevant thresholds if the increase occurs through an acquisition or an allotment of voting securities which is approved by an ordinary resolution of shareholders of the Code company. An ordinary resolution is a resolution passed at a meeting of the disinterested holders of voting securities of the Code company by a simple majority of the votes of those holders who voted on the resolution (excluding the person acquiring the voting securities).

6.3.6 Compulsory Acquisition

[215] If a person (or persons acting jointly and in concert) becomes the holder or controller of more than 90% of shares in a Code company, they are deemed to be a 'dominant owner'. The key consequences of becoming a dominant owner are:

- the dominant owner has the right to compulsorily acquire the remaining equity securities in the Code company; and
- the holders of the outstanding securities have the right to sell those securities to the dominant owner.

[216] If an Offeror becomes a dominant owner by reason of acceptances of a Takeover Offer, the Offeror may compulsorily acquire all remaining shares by giving an acquisition notice within twenty working days after the end of the offer period. The consideration payable must be the same as the consideration provided under the Takeover Offer (with certain exceptions).

[217] If an Offeror becomes a dominant owner otherwise than via a Takeover Offer, the Offeror may also compulsorily acquire all remaining shares by giving an acquisition notice within twenty working days of becoming a dominant owner. The consideration payable must be a cash sum and is typically certified as fair and reasonable by an independent adviser. Where a certain level of shareholders objects to the proposed consideration, it will be determined by an independent expert appointed by the Panel.

6.4 Takeover Offers

6.4.1 Same Terms and Consideration

[218] It is a requirement of the Takeovers Code that an offer must be made on the same terms and provide the same consideration for all securities belonging to the same class of equity securities under offer. No differential treatment of shareholders is permitted.

6.4.2 Conditions

[219] A Takeover Offer may be subject to any condition, so long as the condition is not under control, or dependant on the judgment, of the Offeror (or any associate of the Offeror) or the fulfilment of which is in power, or under the control, of the Offeror (or any associate of the Offeror). For example, a Takeover Offer cannot be made conditional on satisfactory due diligence being conducted by the Offeror.

[220] An offer which is subject to conditions must specify a date by which an offer is to become unconditional. An Offeror must not allow an offer to lapse in unreasonable reliance on a condition.

6.4.3 Independent Adviser's Report

[221] The directors of the Code company subject to a Takeover Offer must obtain a report from an independent adviser on the merits of the offer which is provided to shareholders before voting on the offer.

[222] The independent adviser's report will typically include a valuation range for the securities the subject of the Takeover Offer. In determining the merits of an offer, both value-based and non-value-based factors may be taken into account by the independent adviser.

[223] In addition, where an offer is being made for multiple classes of equity securities, the Offeror must obtain a report from an independent adviser certifying that, in the adviser's opinion, the offer is fair and reasonable between classes.

6.4.4 Defensive Tactics

[224] The Takeovers Code restricts a Code company from taking or permitting any action, in relation to the affairs of a Code company, which could effectively result in a Takeover Offer being frustrated or the holders of equity securities of a Code company being denied an opportunity to decide on the merits of an offer, commonly known as defensive tactics. The restriction on defensive tactics is triggered when the Target company has received a Takeover Notice or has reason to believe a bona fide offer is imminent. The restriction will therefore be triggered in some instances before a Takeover Notice is received.

[225] These restrictions do not apply in certain circumstances, including where the action is approved by shareholders or where the action is taken or permitted for reasons unrelated to the Takeover Offer with the approval from the Panel. These restrictions do not prevent the directors of the Target company from encouraging a genuine competing offer from another potential Offeror.

6.4.5 Procedure for Making a Takeover Offer

[226]

- *Takeover Notice*: To commence a Takeover Offer under the Code, an Offeror must send a Takeover Notice to the Target company. The Takeover Notice is a statement of the Offeror's intention to make an offer (*Takeover Notice*). Although the notice does not constitute the offer itself, the Takeover Notice must include the proposed terms and conditions of the offer. The Takeover Notice must be given to the Panel and the NZX (if the Target company is listed) at the same time as it is given to the Target, and at least ten working days before the offer document is sent to shareholders.
- *Disclosure*: If the Target is a listed issuer, immediately upon receipt of a Takeover Notice, it must send to the licensed market operator a copy of the Takeover Notice. If the Target is not a listed issuer, immediately upon receipt of a Takeover Notice, it must do all that is reasonably practicable to ensure shareholders are given notice in writing of the Takeover Notice. The Target is also required to send to the Offeror, a 'class notice' which contains a description of its equity securities.
- *Offer document*: The Offeror must send the offer document to all holders of securities on the Target company's register between ten working days and twenty working days after the Takeover Notice is sent to the Target company (if the Offeror still wishes to proceed with the offer). The Takeovers Code prescribes certain information which must be included in the offer document. After sending the offer document, the Offeror must notify the Target company and the licensed market operator by providing a 'despatch notice'.
- *Target's response*: Under the Takeovers Code, the Target is required to respond to the Offeror in the form of a 'Target company statement' within the ten working days after the Target has received the Takeover Notice or within ten working days of the Target receiving the despatch notice. The Target company statement will typically include a recommendation from the Target

company's directors as to whether they recommend shareholders to accept the offer or not.

- *Offer period*: The offer period must remain open for no less than twenty working days and, generally, no longer than sixty working days. An Offeror may vary the offer to extend the offer period, provided the amended period does not exceed sixty working days (with certain exceptions).

6.5 Schemes of Arrangement

6.5.1 Overview

[227] Schemes provide an alternative structure to that of a Takeover Offer to acquire Code companies. The use of Schemes in New Zealand has become increasingly common in recent years following legislative changes and increased market acceptance and familiarity with this transaction structure.

[228] A Scheme is a court-supervised process under which the court has broad discretion to order that a reorganisation of the share capital of a company will be binding on that company and any other person that the court thinks fit (including the Target shareholders). Accordingly, Schemes may be used to effect a wide range of corporate restructures, including transfers of all of each shareholders' securities to an Offeror.

[229] Schemes have the added advantage of being an 'all or nothing' outcome. The Offeror will have the certainty of knowing that it will either acquire 100% control of the Target if the Scheme is successful or nothing if the Scheme is unsuccessful.

6.5.2 Shareholder Voting Thresholds

[230] For a Scheme to be approved by Target shareholders, it needs to be approved by:

- at least 75% of the votes of the shareholders in each interest class entitled to vote and voting on the Scheme; and
- a simple majority of the votes of shareholders entitled to vote (i.e., more than half of the votes attached to all shares on issue, whether they are voted or not).

[231] If the Scheme is approved by the requisite majorities (and satisfies all other conditions, including court approval), it will become binding on all Target shareholders (including on those shareholders who voted against the Scheme or did not vote at the Scheme meeting). Consequently, an Offeror may acquire 100% control of the Target if these thresholds are met, which contrasts with a Takeover Offer, where at least 90% of acceptances are required before a bidder can acquire the remaining securities through the compulsory acquisition route.

6.5.3 The Court's Role

[232] The court's overarching role is to ensure the scheme is implemented in accordance with the Companies Act.

[233] The court's approval is required at two stages of a scheme transaction. At the initial court hearing, the Target will seek the court's approval to send the Scheme booklet to its shareholders and to convene the 'Scheme meeting' at which its shareholders will vote on the Scheme. At the final court hearing (which is held after the Scheme has been approved by shareholders), the Target will seek 'final orders' from the court to approve the Scheme.

[234] The Companies Act provides that the court may not approve a Scheme unless the requisite voting thresholds (described above) have been met and either the:

- court is satisfied that the shareholders of the Target will not be adversely affected by the use of the Scheme rather than a Takeover Offer to effect the acquisition of the Target; or
- Target has filed a statement from the Panel indicating that the Panel has no objection to an order being made to approve the Scheme.

[235] It is important to note, however, that the court has a general discretion whether or not to approve the Scheme. A court may refuse to sanction a Scheme (or convene the Scheme meeting) if it considers the Scheme will potentially prejudice shareholders, creditors or other parties, even if the requisite voting thresholds have been met at the Scheme meeting.

6.5.4 The Panel's Role

[236] The Panel's role on a scheme is to assist the court in determining whether or not relevant matters have been brought to the court's attention as part of the court considering whether or not to approve the Scheme. The Panel will review Scheme documentation to ensure that appropriate disclosures are made to shareholders, that interest classes have been adequately identified and that appropriate shareholder protections are in place.

[237] The Panel is typically requested by the Target to provide a 'no-objection statement' in relation to the Scheme, which the Target will use to support its Scheme application to the court.

6.5.5 Interest Classes

[238] The Companies Act requires that a Scheme must be considered and voted on by each interest class affected by it. It is therefore important to identify all interest classes from the outset of the transaction. An interest class is, broadly speaking, a group of shareholders with similar rights against the Target. Interest classes for the purposes of New Zealand Schemes are to be determined in accordance with the

principles set out in the Companies Act, including whether shareholders legal rights are:

- so dissimilar that they cannot sensibly consult together about a common interest will be in different interest classes;
- sufficiently similar that they can consult together about a common interest will be in the same interest class; or
- different under a proposed arrangement or amalgamation, then those shareholders are in different interest classes.

[239] The Panel expects the division of classes to be clearly disclosed in the Scheme documents, together with an explanation of why the divisions have been drawn. Equally, the court will need to be certain the interest classes have been correctly determined before approving the Scheme.

6.5.6 Key Stages of a Scheme

[240] The following are the key stages of an acquisition of a Code company implemented by way of Scheme:

- *Scheme implementation agreement*: the initial stage of a Scheme typically involves the Offeror and the Target negotiating and entering into a 'Scheme implementation agreement' which sets out the terms and conditions of the transaction. The Offeror will typically conduct due diligence in parallel to this process.
- *Panel review*: the Target will typically share a draft of the Scheme booklet and notice of shareholders' meeting to be sent to shareholders with the Panel for its review and seek a 'no-objections statement'.
- *Initial court hearing*: at the initial court hearing, the Target will seek consent orders from the Court, approving the despatch of the Scheme booklet and the convening of the Scheme meeting.
- *Scheme meeting*: the Target's shareholders will vote on whether to approve the Scheme at the Scheme meeting.
- *Final court hearing*: if the Scheme is approved by the Target's shareholders, the Target will seek 'final orders' from the court to approve the Scheme at the final court hearing.
- *Implementation:* within a specified number of days after the final court hearing, the Scheme becomes effective.

6.5.7 Other Considerations

[241] The commentary in sections 6.4.2 (conditions), 6.4.3 (the Independent Adviser's Report), 6.4.4 (defensive tactics) and 6.3.3 (associates) apply equally to Schemes.

7 OVERSEAS INVESTMENT

7.1 Overview

[242] The Overseas Investment Act 2005 (the *Overseas Investment Act*) regulates certain acquisitions of sensitive assets, particularly land, in New Zealand by overseas persons. The purpose of the Overseas Investment Act is to:

- recognise that it is a privilege for an overseas person to own or control sensitive New Zealand assets and accordingly require any investment in such assets to meet certain criteria before it can be made, and make such investment subject to ongoing conditions; and
- manage certain risks, such as national security and public order risks associated with transactions by overseas persons.

[243] Sensitive acquisitions will require the approval of the OIO before the overseas person can make such an investment. Due to the criteria which must be met and the timeframes associated with obtaining OIO approval, an analysis of whether the Overseas Investment Act applies to a proposed transaction is a key step to be undertaken early when considering an acquisition in New Zealand.

7.2 Overseas Persons

[244] The starting point is to consider whether the acquisition will be made by an overseas person. Primarily, an 'overseas person' is a:

(1) person who is not a New Zealand citizen nor ordinarily resident in New Zealand; or
(2) body corporate that is:
  - incorporated outside of New Zealand;
  - more than 25% owned by a body corporate incorporated outside New Zealand; or
  - more than 25% controlled by a body corporate incorporated outside New Zealand (including through the power to control the governing body of that body corporate or exercise voting rights).

[245] Accordingly, a New Zealand incorporated special purpose vehicle that is beneficially owned by overseas persons will still be an 'overseas person' and cannot circumvent this regime.

[246] 'Associates' of overseas persons are also caught. This definition is broad and is intended to capture a wide variety of relationships. When considering if a person is an associate of the overseas person, it does not matter whether the control, power, influence, arrangement or relationship is direct or indirect, general or specific, or legally enforceable or not.

7.3 Significant Business Assets

[247] An overseas investment in 'significant business assets' will require the approval of the OIO. An acquisition of significant business assets includes an overseas person, or an associate of an overseas person:

- acquiring an interest in assets or securities which will result in the overseas person acquiring more than 25% ownership or control interest of a person, or increasing an existing ownership or control interest above 25%, if the value or consideration exceeds NZD100 m;
- establishing a business in New Zealand where total expenditure expected to be incurred before commencing that business exceeds NZD100 m; or
- acquiring other property (such as goodwill or intangible assets) in New Zealand that is used to carry on business in New Zealand if the total value of the consideration exceeds NZD100 m.

[248] However, higher monetary thresholds for 'significant business assets' may apply for:

- certain Australian non-government investors, increasing the threshold to NZD536 m for 2020 (the threshold is adjusted for inflation each year); or
- certain investors from specified Asia-Pacific countries with whom New Zealand has relevant trade agreements, increasing the threshold to NZD200 m.

[249] To obtain consent to acquire significant business assets, applicants must meet the 'investor test' by providing the OIO with evidence that:

(1) they are financially committed to the transaction (e.g., by providing details of funding for the acquisition or other expenses incurred in preparing for the acquisition); and
(2) the 'individuals with control' of the relevant overseas persons involved in the transaction are:
   - of 'good character' (e.g., that the person has not been convicted of, or subject to a credible investigation relating to, a criminal offence); and
   - have sufficient business experience and acumen.

7.4 Sensitive Land

[250] An overseas investment in 'sensitive land' will also require the approval of the OIO. The acquisition of 'sensitive land' must result in an overseas person, or an associate of the overseas person, acquiring rights or an interest in that sensitive land which gives it a more than 25% ownership or control interest or increases an existing ownership or control interest above 25%. An interest in land includes either owning the freehold interest or leasing it for a term of three years or more.

[251] Sensitive land includes a broad range of types of land, such as:

- residential land;
- non-urban land greater than five hectares;
- land including waterways, such as the foreshore, seabed, a lake or river;
- conservation, historic, public reserves or land of cultural significance;
- forestry rights exceeding 1,000 hectares in a calendar year; and
- also captures land which adjoins certain types of sensitive land.

[252] Other than for residential land, identifying sensitive land is highly technical and requires assessment by legal practitioners.

[253] To obtain consent to acquire sensitive land, overseas persons must satisfy the OIO that the investment will benefit New Zealand (in some cases, the identified benefits of the investment must be substantial). When considering whether benefits to New Zealand exist, consideration will be given to matters including whether the investment will, or is likely to, result in new jobs, introduce new technology or skills, increase competition, increase exports or result in additional investment. Additional considerations will also apply depending on the type of sensitive land (e.g., measures for protecting conservation, undertaking maintenance or restoration and public walking access).

[254] Additional requirements for the sales process also apply to acquisitions of:

- farm land, which must first be offered for sale on the open market; and
- land with special features, such as significant bodies of water, which must be first offered to the Crown to purchase.

[255] If the target land is sensitive because it is residential, the overseas person may also seek consent under three additional pathways, which generally require the achievement of certain developmental or other business-related outcomes on the land or commitment by the relevant overseas person to reside permanently in New Zealand.

[256] At the time of writing, the Overseas Investment Act is undergoing reform which is proposed to amend the sensitive land regime.

7.5 The 'National Interest Test' and Call-In Regime

7.5.1 National Interest Test

[257] The New Zealand Government has recently introduced a new 'national interest' assessment which enables it to review certain types of significant transactions which are relevant to the national interest of New Zealand. Transactions subject to the national interest assessment will be those relating to land or assets used for strategically important business, or involving investors associated with foreign governments.

[258] 'Strategically important businesses' to which the national interest test will apply include those involved in ports or airports, electricity generation or distribution, water infrastructure, or telecommunications infrastructure or services, as well as critical direct suppliers to the defence force, media businesses with significant impact, and financial institutions, or any other business in a strategically important industry or that owns or controls high-risk national infrastructure. The relevant Government Minister also has discretion to determine whether any other investment in significant business assets or sensitive land is of the national interest.

[259] In carrying out the national interest assessment, the relevant Minister assessing the transaction may consider the impact of the investment on New Zealand's national security, economic and social development, and general alignment of the transaction with New Zealand's values and interests, and may decline consent if it considers the transaction is contrary to any of these factors.

7.5.2 Temporary Notification

[260] In the wake of COVID-19, the New Zealand Government introduced a temporary requirement that overseas persons notify the OIO of certain acquisitions that may not otherwise have required OIO approval. A notification is required for:

(1) *New Zealand businesses*: any transactions (irrespective of value) that result in an overseas person:
   - acquiring an interest in a New Zealand business of more than 25%; or
   - increasing an existing interest in a New Zealand business up to or beyond the thresholds of 50%, 75% or 100%; and

(2) *Assets*: any transaction where an overseas person acquires more than 25% of the value of the seller's New Zealand business assets (irrespective of the value of that transaction).

7.5.3 Call-in Regime

[261] Once the temporary notification regime is no longer considered to be necessary by the New Zealand Government, it will be replaced by a new call-in regime.

[262] This regime will give the OIO powers to 'call-in' for review certain overseas investments in strategically important business assets that would not otherwise require consent. For example, an investment by an overseas person that was valued at less than NZD100 m and did not exceed any ownership thresholds for significant business assets consent could still be 'called in' for review by the OIO if the target was a strategically important business in New Zealand.

[263] Transactions called in for assessment under this regime will then be assessed to determine whether they give rise to national security and public order risks. If a transaction is found to be contrary to the national interest, the relevant Minister may block the transaction or make the acquisition subject to any conditions that the relevant Minister thinks appropriate in the circumstances to manage any risks associated with the investment.

7.6 Application Process

7.6.1 Costs

[264] Fees for most overseas investment applications range from NZD32 000 for significant business assets only to NZD54 000 for both significant business assets and sensitive land, with an additional NZD54 000 fee if a national interest assessment is required. Filing a notification under the temporary regime does not incur any fees to the OIO. At the time of writing, fees are subject to review, with a substantial increase possible.

7.6.2 Timeframes for Assessment

[265] The time needed to prepare an OIO application varies, but investors should be aware that substantial information may be required, particularly for acquisitions in certain types of sensitive land, and allow adequate time to prepare this application.

[266] The OIO does not have a statutory time frame within which it must respond to an OIO application. Instead, this will vary depending on the level and quality of information included in the initial application and the complexity of the proposed acquisition. In general:

- assessment timeframes for notifications under the temporary regime range from ten to seventy business days, although the majority of these are expected to be assessed within ten working days;
- it takes approximately three months to obtain consent for an acquisition of significant business assets or residential land only;
- it can be expected to take up to five months for other sensitive land; and
- consent applications subject to the national interest test or that must be reviewed by the relevant Minister for other reasons (e.g., because they involve non-urban land over five hectares) may take up to six months to review or longer where significant issues are identified.

[267] The acquisition cannot be implemented until OIO approval is received.

7.6.3 Conditions

[268] The Overseas Investment Act imposes two 'automatic conditions' on every consent granted, being that:

- the information provided by the applicant was correct at the time it was provided; and
- each consent holder must comply with the representations and plans they made in support of the application and which were notified by the OIO as having been taken into account when consent was granted (unless compliance should reasonably be excused).

[269] In addition, if the transaction is of the 'national interest', it will be an 'automatic condition' that each consent holder must not, in relation to sensitive assets in which the relevant investment is made, act or omit to act with a purpose or an intention of adversely affecting national security or public order.

[270] The OIO may also impose other conditions considered to be appropriate, and if the OIO is likely to grant consent, it will issue draft consent conditions for the applicant to comment on before the OIO or relevant Ministers make a decision. In the case of:

- 'significant business assets' applications, conditions commonly include reporting requirements and a requirement that the individuals with control of the asset remain of good character; and
- 'sensitive land' applications, consent conditions will likely require an applicant to introduce the benefits claimed in the application. For example, if one of the claimed benefits of the transaction is a certain number of new jobs, the OIO may make the creation of those jobs a condition of consent and subsequently monitor and enforce that condition. It is therefore important that an applicant carefully considers the nature of the benefits it identifies and claims in their application.

[271] Once conditions have been imposed and consent granted, the applicant must meet those conditions. If the applicant subsequently fails to meet a condition of their consent, they may be required to dispose of the land and/or be subject to fines or other penalties.

7.7 Enforcement

[272] While historically there have not been a large number of cases of enforcement under the Overseas Investment Act, enforcement is an increasing priority of the OIO. The OIO's current strategic priorities[17] for enforcement include, if a benefit was an important factor to granting consent and this is not delivered, if the overseas person deliberately or recklessly breaches the rules or tries to disguise their behaviour, failure to obtain consent (particularly if consent is unlikely to have been granted), overseas persons who make significant gains (such as property speculation) and public harm is created (such as environmental damage).

[273] An overseas person who gives effect to a transaction before being granted the required consent under the Overseas Investment Act commits an offence and is liable on conviction in the case of:

- an individual, to imprisonment for a term of up to twelve months or a maximum fine of NZD300 000; and
- a company or any other entity, a maximum fine of NZD300 000.

[17] OIO enforcement function and strategic priorities, https://www.linz.govt.nz/overseas-investment/enforcement/oio-enforcement-function-and-strategic-priorities.

[274] The OIO's consent will be subject to conditions and a person who fails to comply with any such condition, without lawful excuse, commits an offence and is liable on conviction to a fine not exceeding NZD100 000.

[275] A court may also order a person who breaches the Overseas Investment Act to pay a civil pecuniary penalty to the Crown or any other person (so long as that person has not also been required to pay a fine for that same conduct). The maximum civil pecuniary penalties for breaching the Overseas Investment Act is capped at NZD500 000 for an individual and NZD10 m for corporates and other entities.

[276] Further, the OIO can make orders requiring disposal of property acquired in breach of the Overseas Investment Act.

7.8 Fishing

[277] The OIO administers the provisions of the Fisheries Act 1996 relating to overseas investment in fishing quota or an interest in fishing quota. Under these provisions, any transaction which results in an overseas investment in fishing quota will require consent. Applicants for consent to acquire fishing quota must also satisfy the national interest test.

7.9 Forestry and Forestry Rights

[278] Acquisitions by an overseas person of forestry rights relating to over 1,000 hectares in a calendar year will constitute an acquisition of 'sensitive land' under the Overseas Investment Act and require consent. Acquisitions of other profits-à-prendre (other than those relating to minerals) will require consent where these relate to land that is considered 'sensitive' under the Overseas Investment Act.

[279] Overseas investors can apply to the OIO for consent using one of three forestry consent pathways. The first and most complex pathway is the standard 'benefits test' (which is the same test applied to other categories of sensitive land, aside from residential land). Consistent with the New Zealand Government's aim to increase tree numbers, one key prerequisite to qualifying for either of the following two alternative pathways is that a new crop of trees is planted to replace any that are harvested. Provided this (and limited additional) criteria are satisfied, overseas investors may apply for consent under either a 'modified benefits test' or the 'special forestry test' (e.g., if there are pre-existing beneficial activities such as environmental protections in place). The Overseas Investment Act also allows for investors in forestry to seek 'standing consents'.

7.10 Restrictions on Overseas Directors/Managers

[280] A New Zealand company can have any number of non-New Zealand directors or managers, provided that it all New Zealand companies must have at least one local director. In addition to the standard qualifications which apply to all directors (*see* section 3.3 of this chapter), a local director is one who lives in:

- New Zealand, or
- Australia, and who is a director of a company incorporated in Australia.

[281] Generally, a person will be considered to live in New Zealand if they are present in New Zealand for more than 183 days in a 12 month period. However, the Registrar for Companies can consider other persons to be living in New Zealand even if this is not the case in some circumstances (e.g., if that person can show other connection and ties to New Zealand).

8 MERGER CONTROL

8.1 Overview of Commerce Act

[282] New Zealand's merger control regime is governed by the Commerce Act 1986 (the *Commerce Act*). The Commerce Act (among other things) aims to promote competition in New Zealand markets for the long-term benefit of consumers by prohibiting certain conduct and business arrangements, including acquisitions of business assets or shares, that have the purpose or effect of substantially lessening competition within the market concerned. The New Zealand Commerce Commission (the *Commission*) is the independent statutory authority responsible for merger control in New Zealand.

[283] In New Zealand there is no compulsory requirement to notify the Commission of business acquisitions. Instead, a purchaser can voluntarily submit proposed acquisitions to the Commission for review if a proposed acquisition may result in a substantial lessening of competition in a market.

8.2 Substantial Lessening of Competition

[284] The Commerce Act prohibits a person (or interconnected and associated persons) from acquiring the assets or shares of a business, if the acquisition would have, or would be likely to have, the effect of substantially lessening competition in a market in New Zealand. 'Likely' has been interpreted by the courts as meaning 'a real chance', which is a relatively low threshold, given the everyday meaning of 'likely' is more akin to 'probable'.

8.2.1 Threshold

[285] There is no set minimum acquisition threshold below which the Commission will not assess whether a substantial lessening of competition could occur. This is determined by reference to the 'substantial degree of influence' test, which can apply to interests of much less than 50%.

[286] If the merger does not result in an aggregation of market share in any market in New Zealand (and the purchaser or target is not an actual or potential entrant into any market in which the other party operates and there are no anti-competitive vertical integration issues or conglomerate effects), the acquisition will not result in a substantial lessening of competition. The Commission's Guidelines provide 'indicators' of when a transaction would be likely not to raise competition concerns:

- where post-merger the three largest firms in the market have a combined market share of less than 70%, and the merged firm's market share is less than 40%; or
- where post-merger the three largest firms in the market have a combined market share of 70% or more, and the merged firm's market share is less than 20%.

[287] These concentration indicators are provided in the Commission's Guidance as 'initial guides' and are explicitly not exemptions or safe harbours. Similarly, there is no assumption that a transaction not satisfying these thresholds will substantially lessen competition.

8.2.2 Effect of Clearance

[288] As noted above, seeking clearance is voluntary. If it is sought and granted, clearance has the benefit of providing an assurance that the Commission will not open an investigation into the transaction of its own initiative at a later date. If the Commission grants clearance for a transaction, neither it nor third parties can subsequently challenge the proposed transaction in court.

[289] If an application for clearance is not made, and the Commission subsequently forms the view that the transaction would result in a likely substantial lessening of competition, it can seek an injunction to prevent the transaction from completing. While the regime is non-suspensory, completing during the Commission's review will terminate the approval process, and if completion occurs before clearance is granted, the Commission may open an investigation.

8.2.3 Offshore Acquisitions

[290] The Commission may also make an application to the High Court for a declaration in respect of overseas acquisitions that result in acquisition of a New Zealand body corporate where that acquisition has, or is likely to have, the effect of substantially lessening competition in a market in New Zealand. If such a declaration is made, the court may make an order requiring the New Zealand body corporate to cease carrying on business in New Zealand in the market to which the declaration relates within six months, dispose of shares or other assets, or take any other actions that the court considers appropriate. A declaration must be made within twelve months after the acquisition, and cannot be made if the Commission has already given a clearance or granted an authorisation for the acquisition.

8.3 Notification Process

8.3.1 Pre-notification Discussions

[291] While not mandatory, the Commission encourages parties to engage in pre-notification discussions with the Commission in order to ensure the application contains all required information and the Commission case team is able to conduct its review as quickly as possible. Pre-notification discussions generally run for around one to three weeks but can reduce clearance timeframes and information requests. However, ultimately, the timeframe will depend on the complexity of issues identified and whether there is opposition to the acquisition. The Commission treats pre-notification as confidential and no announcements are made during pre-notification without the consent of the notifying parties.

8.3.2 Clearance Applications

[292] The purchaser is responsible for filing a notice seeking clearance if such a filing is deemed appropriate. Parties wishing to seek clearance should ensure that their sale and purchase agreement is conditional on receipt of clearance.

[293] Once the Commission has registered a clearance application, it will issue a media release and publish a statement of preliminary issues (SOPI). The Commission does this to inform the public of the proposed merger and to gather information from interested parties. Upon publication of the SOPI, the Commission invites interested parties, including trade competitors and other stakeholders, to provide comment on the likely competitive effects of the proposed acquisition. The Commission will also actively seek input from potentially interested parties, which it will collect via interviews.

[294] Clearance for relatively straightforward transactions can be granted within forty working days. This timeframe can be extended with the consent of the applicants as clearance is deemed to be declined if the Commission has not reached a decision by the due date. Current experience suggests parties should expect approximately forty to sixty working days for a relatively straightforward clearance. However, this can extend to six months or more for a complex matter.

[295] In the context of bids for publicly held companies, the implications of the clearance process on transaction timing can vary. Where the transaction involves a scheme of arrangement, timeframes are generally flexible, allowing for a clearance process of almost any length without issue. However, the takeover regime in New Zealand is much more rigid, meaning the clearance process can cause difficulty if it cannot be aligned with the maximum timeframes stipulated for a takeover under the Takeovers Code. The Commission is generally reluctant to provide any guarantees to filing parties on timing, so it may be difficult to get clearances finalised exactly in accordance with the takeover process, particularly given the practical difficulty of not being able to advance an application meaningfully before announcement of the transaction given the Commission's typical requirement that it make public enquiries about the effect of the transaction.

8.3.3 Authorisations

[296] Where parties consider that a transaction may result in a substantial lessening of competition, but that the 'detriments' of the lessening of competition are outweighed by the 'benefits', they can apply to the Commission for 'authorisation' of the transaction. This is a separate process from applying for clearance.

[297] Authorisations are relatively uncommon, costly and can be time consuming. This process is unlikely to be relevant to a global transaction with a New Zealand component.

8.3.4 Divestments Undertakings

[298] Where a transaction raises competition concerns, the purchaser can provide an undertaking to sell certain assets or shares as a condition of clearance in order to remedy those competition concerns if such a divestment results in additional competitive constraints such that a substantial lessening of competition is no longer likely. The Commission can only accept structural undertakings to divest assets of shares, and cannot accept behavioural undertakings.

8.4 Sanctions for Breaching the Merger Control Laws

[299] If an actual or potential transaction has the effect or likely effect of substantially lessening competition in a market in New Zealand, courts can impose penalties of up to NZD5 m on a body corporate and NZD500 000 on individuals. A seller can also be liable. The Commission must seek such penalties for a breach of the merger control provisions within three years of when the matter giving rise to the breach arose.

[300] In addition to monetary penalties, if an acquiring firm does not apply to the Commission for a clearance or an authorisation and the transaction is in breach of section 47, the Commission may apply to the High Court seeking an injunction to prevent the acquisition occurring. Courts can also impose other orders, including orders for the divestiture of assets or shares. Third parties can seek damages.

9 INDUSTRY SPECIFIC REGULATION

9.1 Overview

[301] As described in section 7.5 of this chapter, investment by an overseas person in a 'strategically important business' will require the approval of the OIO under the national interest test. 'Strategically important businesses' include those involved in ports or airports, electricity generation or distribution, water infrastructure, or telecommunications infrastructure or services, as well as critical direct suppliers to the defence force, media businesses with significant impact, and financial institutions, or any other business in a strategically important industry or that owns or controls high-risk national infrastructure. In addition, the OIO regulates investments in the fishing and forestry industry as well.

[302] In addition to OIO approvals:

- operating a business in certain industries requires a particular licence or permit be granted and, where the conditions of those licences relate to ownership, control or management, the acquisition of a business may require confirmation from a regulatory authority that the licence can continue; and
- specific regulatory approvals are required for an investment in particular industries, whether the investment is by an overseas person or a New Zealander.

[303] Below is a summary of these requirements in key industries.

9.2 Banks

[304] The Reserve Bank of New Zealand (the RBNZ) registers and supervises banks in New Zealand under the RBNZ Act 1989. Prior written consent of the RBNZ is required if a transaction would result in the person (whether foreign or domestic) acquiring 'significant influence' in the bank, being:

- the ability to directly or indirectly appoint 25% or more of the board of directors (or other persons exercising powers of management, however described) of the bank; or
- acquiring a direct or indirect qualifying interest in 10% or more of the voting shares of the bank.

[305] The RBNZ may specify the level of significant influence which may be acquired by that person without the need for further consents and make its consent subject to such terms and conditions that the RBNZ thinks fit.

[306] If a person already has acquired a significant influence over the bank (with consent from the RBNZ) and the proposed transaction would result in increasing the level of significant influence beyond what has already been permitted, a further consent from the RBNZ will be required.

9.3 Non-bank Deposit Takers

[307] A non-bank deposit taker (NBDT) is defined as including persons who offer debt securities to the public and carry on the business of borrowing and lending money and/or provide financial services. The registration and governance of NBDTs is by the NBDTs Act 2013, which is supervised by the RBNZ. Under the NBDT Act, every NBDT must be licenced to undergo any deposit-taking activities. The RBNZ is the regulator in charge of approving licences to NBDTs.

[308] Any person must obtain the RBNZ's written consent prior to completing any transaction which would enable it to acquire or increase its level of influence over an NBDT if that transaction would result in the person:

- having the ability, directly or indirectly, to appoint 25% or more of the members of the NBDT's governing body; or
- having a direct or indirect ownership stake in the NBDT of 20% or more.

[309] In addition, any person who already has the level of control over an NBDT specified above and wishes to increase this level of control must also obtain written consent from the RBNZ.

[310] In considering whether to give permission to this change in control, the RBNZ may specify the level of influence that person may have or acquire over the NBDT without needing further consent, and impose any terms and conditions it deems fit on the consent.

9.4 Insurance

[311] Under the Insurance (Prudential Supervision) Act 2010 (IPS Act), every person who carries on insurance business in New Zealand must have a licence. As with banks and NBDTs, the licencing and regulation of the insurance industry is the RBNZ.

[312] To become the holding entity or obtain a controlling interest of a licenced insurer, prior notification must be given to the RBNZ. Once the RBNZ has received all the necessary information, it must then decide whether it believes that the insurer will continue to satisfy the criteria for the insurer to be issued a licence set out in IPS Act under the control of the potential acquirer. These criteria include, among other things, that it:

- holds a sufficient financial strength rating;
- has the ability to carry on its business in a prudent manner;
- holds and has the ability to maintain a minimum amount of capital in order to meet applicable solvency standards;
- has appropriate policies in place, ensuring appropriate persons met the 'fit and proper' requirements and risk management;

- has an appropriate structure, ownership, governance and financial strength having regard to the size and nature of its business for the types of risk it is proposing to insure.

[313] If the RBNZ is not satisfied that it will meet these requirements after the change of control, the RBNZ may cancel such licence.

9.5 Financial Services

[314] 'Financial services' covers a broad range of services including financial advisers, brokers, building societies, credit providers, credit unions, money changers, finance companies and insurers. All financial service providers in New Zealand must be registered on the Financial Service Providers Register under the Financial Services Providers (Registration and Dispute Resolution) Act 2008 (the FSP Act).

[315] Under the FSP Act, some types of financial services also require a licence to be issued by either the RBNZ or the FMA. The Financial Markets Conduct Act governs the licencing and regulation of market services. Under the Financial Markets Conduct Act, a person will need a licence, subject to certain exceptions, if they are acting as:

- a manager of a registered scheme (other than a restricted scheme);
- an independent trustee of a restricted scheme;
- a provider of a discretionary investment management service; or
- acting as a derivatives issuer in respect of a regulated offer of derivatives.

[316] With the granting of a licence, the Financial Market Conduct Regulations 2014 (the FMC Regulations) impose a general condition to notify the FMA as soon as practicable if certain events occur, which includes matters which may be relevant in an M&A transaction, such as:

- a director, senior manager or any key personnel ceasing to hold the office or position or being appointed, employed or engaged;
- proposing to change their name or legal structure;
- proposing to enter into a major transaction under the meaning given in section 129 of the Companies Act; or
- entering into a transaction or arrangement or is likely to, that will result in a person obtaining or losing control of the licensee or authorised body.

9.6 Oil, Gas and Minerals

[317] Permits are required under the Crown Minerals Act 1991 (the *Crown Minerals Act*) for prospecting, exploring and mining oil, gas and minerals. The permits themselves can be designated either Tier 1 (depending on factors including the type and amount of mineral being mined for) or Tier 2 (which is any permit that does not fall under Tier 1).

[318] Any person, or persons acting jointly, who wishes to or acquires the direct or indirect power to exercise, or control the exercise of, 50% or more of the voting rights in a Tier 1 permit operator will be required to obtain the prior consent of the relevant Minister for the change of control. The consent must include the necessary information including that the permit holder has the financial capability to meet its obligations under the permit, is likely to comply and give proper effect to the work programme for the permit and any relevant obligation under the Crown Minerals Act or any regulations in respect of fees and royalties.

[319] A Tier 2 permit operator is required to notify the relevant Minister if it knows, or ought reasonably to know, that it or a guarantor has undergone a 'change of control'. This notification must be given to the relevant Minister within three months after the permit participant becomes aware, or ought reasonably to have become aware that a change of control has occurred and be accompanied by the necessary documentation that specifies the change of control, a statement from the permit participant and, if applicable, the guarantor, that it has the financial capabilities to meet their respective obligations.

10 DEBT FINANCING

10.1 Common Financing Methods

[320] In the context of a potential acquisition there are numerous financing options available in the New Zealand market. The choice as to the appropriate financing model will depend on multiple factors, including the target and structure of the particular transaction.

[321] With respect to the acquisition of a target business, the financing of the purchase will typically comprise a combination of debt and equity. The debt portion of the purchase price may also be split further into senior and mezzanine funding (usually provided by different lender groups) and additional subordinated debt may be provided by the incoming shareholders.

[322] Where a transaction relates to the acquisition of specific assets, the debt financing may similarly be structured to fund the acquisition of those particular assets (as opposed to the operations of the overall enterprise of the purchaser).

[323] New Zealand has a competitive financing marketplace with local, Australasian and major international financial institutions all participating in financing transactions within New Zealand. The New Zealand debt finance market also encompasses more sophisticated structures, including bond issuances, note placements and securitisation structures.

10.2 Personal Properties and Securities Act

10.2.1 Overview

[324] New Zealand law relating to the taking of security interests in personal property is primarily set out in the Personal Property Securities Act 1999 (the PPSA). The introduction of the PPSA removed the need to distinguish between fixed and floating charges.

[325] The PPSA establishes a regime for the creation of security interests over personal property in favour of creditors over all types of present and future assets of a debtor. However, this security interest does not deprive the debtor of its ability to deal with the relevant property in the ordinary course of business.

[326] Under the PPSA, 'personal property' is broadly defined and most assets owned or used by a business can become subject to a security interest. However, personal property does not include interests in land.

10.2.2 Personal Property Register

[327] The PPSA also established the New Zealand personal property securities register (PPSR). The PPSR is an online publicly searchable register which allows a potential purchaser of assets, or creditor to a business, to search on a debtor to determine whether the assets of that debtor are encumbered by security interests in favour of other parties.

[328] Under the PPSA there are two steps that must be completed to obtain a perfected security interest:

- *attachment*: a security interest attaches to an asset when value is given by the secured party, the debtor acquires rights in the assets and the debtor has signed a security agreement; and
- *perfection*: perfection means that a secured party has taken the necessary steps to protect its security interest in assets against competing claims. This is typically achieved through registration of a financing statement on the PPSR, but there are also other methods of perfection for certain asset classes.

[329] The combination of attachment and perfection gives a secured party the rights in the assets which it can enforce against the debtor and third parties.

10.2.3 Registration of Security Interest

[330] Typically the time of registration of a financing statement on the PPSR will determine relative priority between competing creditors (subject to certain exceptions, including if contractual priority arrangements are agreed). As such, for a secured party financing an acquisition the registration of financing statements on the PPSR should be completed as soon as possible and, if possible, prior to funding the acquisition of the relevant assets/shares.

[331] In certain circumstances the security interest to be taken by a secured party financing the acquisition of specific assets may qualify as a 'purchase money security interest', which would provide that secured party with super priority as against other creditors in relation to those assets (subject to satisfaction of the qualifying criteria, including as to the timing of registrations).

[332] It is important to note that a financing statement will automatically expire five years after its date of registration. To maintain the original priority, the financing statement must be renewed before it expires.

10.2.4 Real Property

[333] As noted above, personal property does not include interests in land. Instead, a lender may register a mortgage on New Zealand's centralised electronic land registry, Land Information New Zealand (LINZ). Priority is determined by the point in time of registration. All registered interests will gain priority over unregistered mortgages, even if there is knowledge of the existence of an unregistered interest.

10.2.5 Completion Mechanics in M&A Transaction

[334] Typically, a seller will be required under the sale and purchase agreement to discharge all encumbrances over the relevant shares or assets, on or prior to completion (although encumbrances in the ordinary course of business (such as for leased equipment) may remain in place). The purchaser should obtain a signed deed of release in respect of any security interest in the shares or assets, and a verification statement evidencing the discharge from the PPSR of any financing statements registered in respect of the shares or assets or an amendment of the financing statement so that the collateral description clearly no longer includes the relevant shares or assets.

[335] New Zealand companies do not typically have certificated shares, as such a lender financing an acquisition of shares in a target company (and taking security over such shares) would typically complete the necessary registrations on the PPSR, require that their security interest is noted on the share register of the target company and that they are delivered a blank, signed share transfer form in relation to such shares (to be used should they enforce their security interest).

10.3 Enforcement and Insolvency

[336] The enforcement process in New Zealand is relatively straightforward and typically private in nature. There are several insolvency regimes in New Zealand that could apply to a body corporate incorporated in New Zealand, being liquidation, administration, statutory management, receivership and creditor compromise.

[337] In circumstances where a party wishes to initiate enforcement of a security interest or an insolvency action against a body corporate, the most suitable option will depend on several factors, including the type of body corporate that will be the subject of the enforcement proceedings, the nature of the security that has been granted (if any) and the provisions included in any relevant documentation (including any security agreements).

[338] In any liquidation of a body corporate's assets, there are certain creditor claims that must be paid out in preference to the claims of other creditors. The Companies Act specifies the order of priority and includes claims with priorities relating to the expenses of liquidation, employee entitlements and claims of the Inland Revenue Department (IRD). However, the assets from which preferential claims are to be paid from do not include company assets which are subject to a security interest. This means that (subject to certain exceptions relating to accounts receivable and/or inventory) secured creditors take priority over those creditors with claims arising under the Companies Act.

[339] In addition, a liquidator may look to challenge certain transactions that occurred prior to the commencement of the liquidation. Broadly, a transaction may be prone to challenge as voidable if it occurred:

- *preferential transactions*: within six months (or two years if the transaction is between related parties) before the commencement of liquidation if, at the time it was entered into, the company could not pay its due debts, and the transaction enabled the person to receive more towards the satisfaction of a debt than they would have received in the liquidation;
- *voidable charges*: within six months (or two years if the transaction is between related parties) before the commencement of liquidation if, immediately after the charge was given, the company was unable to pay its due debts;
- *transactions at an undervalue*: within two years before the commencement of liquidation, if the transaction was at an undervalue and the company was insolvent at the time (or as a result of the transaction); or
- *transactions with directors and others for inadequate or excessive consideration*: within three years of the application to put the company into liquidation for transactions with a director, their relatives, related entities, and others for inadequate or excessive consideration.

[340] Dispositions of property may also be set aside if they are intended to prejudice creditors, if the company is insolvent or in certain other similar circumstances.

11 TAX

11.1 Overview of New Zealand's Tax System

[341] The key legislation governing the imposition and collection of New Zealand tax is the Income Tax Act 2007 (the *Income Tax Act*), the Goods and Services Tax Act

1985 (the *GST Act*) and the Tax Administration Act 1994 (*TA Act*). New Zealand has entered into double tax agreements (DTAs) with its major trading partners, including Australia, Canada, China, Hong Kong, Japan, Singapore, the UK and the United States of America as well as a number of other jurisdictions. The Income Tax Act provides that DTAs have overriding effect in most cases.

[342] New Zealand's tax system is highly transparent. New Zealand's tax rules are primarily contained in the statutes referred to above, with a number of subordinate rules set out in regulations, and determinations issued by the New Zealand IRD, all of which are publicly available.

[343] New Zealand's tax system is relatively certain by international standards. The IRD has the ability to issue binding rulings concerning the tax outcomes of an arrangement. Provided the conditions specified in the ruling are satisfied, the IRD is obliged to follow the ruling. The binding rulings regime can be useful for a taxpayer wanting to obtain certainty as to how the IRD will treat a particular arrangement for tax purposes. The IRD also issues guidance on interpretation of provisions. Compliance by taxpayers with tax rules is a key area of focus for the IRD. In that regard, IRD routinely conducts audits of large corporate taxpayers and in recent years has been active in initiating disputes, particularly where the Commissioner of Inland Revenue considers that a taxpayer may have engaged in a tax avoidance arrangement.

[344] New Zealand's tax system has historically been relatively simple by international standards. For example, as described in further detail below, New Zealand has no comprehensive capital gains tax, goods and services tax (GST) is imposed broadly with only relatively limited exceptions and income tax is imposed on companies at a flat rate of 28%. However, over the last five to ten years, a number of changes to New Zealand's tax rules directed at protecting the tax base against specific structures and situations have been introduced, which has resulted in the New Zealand tax system becoming increasingly complex. Examples are the restricted transfer pricing regime and anti-hybrid rules referred to below.

11.2 Liability to Tax

11.2.1 Liability of Business Vehicles to Income Tax

[345] Income tax is imposed on the taxable income of a taxpayer for each tax year, being their gross income for the year less allowable deductions and net losses carried forward. A company is a taxpayer in its own right. It must therefore file tax returns and pay New Zealand income tax in respect of its taxable income. A 'company' for tax purposes is broadly defined and includes certain unit trusts and foreign limited partnerships with separate legal personality. Companies are currently taxed at a flat rate of 28%. A limited class of closely held companies can elect to be transparent for tax purposes.

[346] New Zealand limited partnerships and overseas limited partnerships which do not have separate legal personality under the law of their formation are generally treated as transparent for New Zealand tax purposes, with taxable income being attributed to the partners in proportion to their partnership share and taxable at the partners' applicable tax rate(s).

11.2.2 Residence and Source

[347] Subject to relief being available under a DTA, New Zealand imposes income tax on a 'residence and source' basis. Under that system:

- a taxpayer who is resident in New Zealand for tax purposes is liable for New Zealand income tax in respect of all its taxable income, whether derived in New Zealand or elsewhere; and
- a non-resident is liable for New Zealand income tax on its taxable income that is derived from New Zealand only.

[348] Thus a non-resident's foreign-sourced income is not part of its assessable income for New Zealand income tax purposes.

[349] A company will be resident in New Zealand where it is incorporated or has its head office in New Zealand, its centre of management is in New Zealand and/or its directors exercise control of the company in New Zealand (even if decision-making also occurs outside New Zealand).

[350] A non-resident enterprise with no New Zealand permanent establishment may be entitled to relief from New Zealand income tax under the 'business profits' article of an applicable DTA. This is provided the non-resident is resident in the counterparty jurisdiction for the purposes of the DTA and is otherwise entitled to the benefit of the DTA.

[351] Where a non-resident enterprise has a New Zealand permanent establishment and a DTA applies, the non-resident's permanent establishment would typically be attributed with the profits which it might be expected to make if it were a distinct and separate enterprise engaged in the same or similar activities, under the same or similar conditions and dealing wholly independently with the non-resident company.

11.2.3 Tax Treatment of Capital Gains

[352] New Zealand does not have a comprehensive capital gains tax. However, there are some situations where gains or losses that might conventionally be regarded as of a capital nature will give rise to taxable income or deductible losses.

[353] Those situations include where personal property (e.g., shares) is disposed of as part of a business of dealing in property of the same or similar type, as part of a profit-making undertaking or scheme or where the relevant property was acquired for the purpose of disposing of it.

[354] A disposal of real property (i.e., land) will be taxable where, among other circumstances, the relevant land was acquired with the intention or purpose of disposing of it, in certain circumstances where the owner or an associate carries on a specified category of business relating to land, or where the land is committed to a qualifying development or subdivision of land, subject to a number of exceptions (e.g., for land which is used as business premises).

[355] The financial arrangements rule also brings to tax certain gains that might otherwise be regarded as capital in nature.

11.2.4 Capital Allowances and Deductions in Respect of Capital Expenditure

[356] Depreciation deductions may be allowed for capital expenditure which gives rise to a depreciable asset. Most tangible assets and certain intangible assets may be depreciated on either a straight-line or diminishing-value basis. The rates of depreciation vary depending on the asset concerned.

[357] Land is not depreciable for tax purposes. Recent legislation reinstated depreciation for non-residential (i.e., commercial) buildings with an estimated useful life of fifty years or more, with effect from the start of the 2021 income year. This reverses the position which existed from the 2012 to 2020 tax years.

[358] Capital expenditure which does not give rise to a depreciable asset is generally non-deductible.

[359] The cost of low-value assets is able to be deducted in the income year of purchase, rather than depreciated over time.

11.2.5 Dividends

[360] Dividends derived by a shareholder are generally taxable income.

[361] The concept of a 'dividend' is broadly defined for income tax purposes. In general, it includes any transfer of value from the company to the recipient caused by a shareholding in the company (irrespective of whether or not this was sourced from retained profits). For example, the transfer of assets to a shareholder at an undervalue, certain bonus share issues and certain share buy-backs all constitute 'dividends'.

[362] New Zealand has an imputation regime which is designed to eliminate double taxation of corporate earnings that New Zealand-resident companies distribute to shareholders. Credit balances in the imputation credit account (ICA) of a company can be used by the company to attach credits to dividends distributed to shareholders. A shareholder's income includes the cash value of the dividend as well as the attached imputation credits, but a credit to the value of the imputation credits is then allowed against the income tax otherwise payable by the shareholder.

11.2.6 Employment Taxes

[363] An employer is required to withhold PAYE from payments of salaries, wages, bonuses and other remuneration provided to its employees. An employer can also elect to withhold PAYE from employee share scheme benefits. An employer which provides certain non-cash benefits (e.g., use of a vehicle or a low interest loan) is required to pay fringe benefit tax in respect of such benefits.

11.2.7 Goods and Services Tax

[364] GST is payable on most supplies of goods and services at a rate of 15%. Some supplies are exempt from GST (e.g., the supply of certain financial services) and some are 'zero-rated', i.e., GST is imposed on the supply at a 0% rate (e.g., the sale of an interest in land in certain circumstances and certain supplies to non-residents).

11.2.8 Stamp Duty and Other Taxes

[365] New Zealand does not have stamp duty, transfer taxes or other similar taxes or duties.

11.3 Tax Considerations Arising in M&A Transactions

11.3.1 Overview

[366] Offshore purchasers in M&A transactions usually require specific advice concerning the tax aspects of the acquisition and funding structure. The optimal structure depends on a variety of factors, including the nature of the assets being acquired (shares or other assets) and if the assets are shares, the percentage of shareholding being acquired under the transaction.

[367] Common considerations include use of a New Zealand resident acquisition company, to facilitate a deduction in New Zealand for interest on acquisition financing against the operating profits of the target company, and maximising the level of interest bearing debt (whether third party or related party) within statutory tolerances. Exit considerations are also important and structuring to ensure robust DTA relief from tax on the proceeds of an exit event are often front of mind.

11.3.2 Share Sale

[368] Unlike an asset sale, a share sale does not result in a step up in the cost base of the target company's underlying assets (except potentially in a case where the target company is exiting a consolidated group).

[369] Further, the purchase of a company's shares does not extinguish any historical tax liabilities of the company. It is therefore common for the purchaser to request an indemnity and warranties in respect of any tax liabilities attributable to periods where the target was owned by the seller. The extent of such an indemnity and warranties is open to negotiation.

[370] The tax outcomes in a share sale are broadly the same for both corporates and individuals. However, a corporate will need to give consideration to the tax treatment of a distribution of the proceeds of a share sale to its shareholder(s).

11.3.3 Asset Sale

[371] In an asset sale, the assets will generally be transferred independent of any historical tax liabilities of the seller or tax relief available to it. It is therefore not usual for warranties or indemnities in respect of tax to be provided by a seller in an asset sale.

[372] The cost base of the assets acquired will usually be reset at the specified purchase price for the purposes of the revenue account property rules and depreciation rules, subject to any specific rules which deem the assets to be disposed of at a particular value. A seller may have tax to pay on income arising from the disposal of the assets, including depreciation recovery (i.e., claw back) income.

[373] At present, tax legislation in New Zealand does not contain general rules as to how the purchase price in an asset sale is to be allocated among the different assets. There are specific rules which require the purchase price to be allocated in a particular way in certain situations. For example, where trading stock is disposed of together with other assets, the seller and purchaser are required to apportion the purchase price between the trading stock and other assets in a way that reflects their respective market values. Where a depreciable asset is disposed of together with other items, the seller is deemed to derive an amount equal to the market value of the depreciable asset.

[374] When purchasing a business as a going concern, goodwill paid for a business is not deductible or depreciable for tax purposes. As a result, it has in the past been common for a purchaser to attempt to have the sale and purchase agreement specifically allocate the purchase price between goodwill and tangible assets.

[375] Purchasers in asset sales have also sometimes sought to structure a New Zealand investment acquisition in such a way as to minimise the amount of non-depreciable goodwill, by providing for apportionment of part of the purchase price to certain depreciable intangible assets.

[376] The allocation of the purchase price in an asset sale is currently an area of interest for the IRD. In recent years, the IRD has become concerned that some sellers and purchasers under asset sales are adopting inconsistent purchase price allocations which do not reflect the market values of the assets being sold in order to gain a tax advantage (e.g., a seller over-allocating a portion of the purchase price to non-taxable goodwill).

[377] The Taxation (Annual Rates for 2020–2021, Feasibility Expenditure, and Remedial Matters) Bill is currently before Parliament. The Bill proposes law changes that, if passed in their current form, would require parties to an asset sale to adopt a consistent approach to allocating the purchase price across the relevant assets and give the IRD the power to adjust such an allocation so that it reflects the respective market values of the assets. The proposed changes would provide the seller with the power to determine the allocation if the parties cannot agree it within a specified period. It is currently proposed that these new rules would apply to asset sale agreements entered into on or after 1 April 2021.

[378] The tax outcomes in an asset sale are broadly the same for both corporates and individuals. However, a corporate will need to give consideration to the tax treatment of a distribution of the proceeds of an asset sale to its shareholder(s).

11.3.4 Revenue Account Property

[379] Where an asset sale includes personal property or land, the seller may be subject to income tax if the revenue account property rules described above apply. A share sale on the other hand does not cause an income tax liability to arise for the seller in respect of revenue account assets held by the target company (except potentially in a case where the target company is exiting a consolidated group).

[380] If the shares in the target company are held on revenue account, a share sale would give rise to a tax liability for the seller. Such a scenario is relatively rare, as share sales typically entail a disposal by a seller of part of the capital structure of its business.

11.3.5 Grouping of Gains and Losses

[381] The ability to carry forward tax losses from one income year to the next is currently based on maintaining a minimum 49% shareholder continuity. Further, a company can potentially offset its tax losses with another group company, but only if there is a minimum 66% commonality of shareholding from the start of the tax year and provided the company in a loss position is not a 'dual resident'. In light of these rules, it is currently difficult to preserve the value of tax losses for use by the purchaser's group post-completion in a share sale scenario.

[382] The New Zealand Government has announced that a 'same or similar business' test for loss carry forward will be introduced, such that a company which fails the continuity requirement above will be able to carry forward tax losses where it continues to carry on the same business or a similar business. Legislation to give effect to this announcement has not yet been introduced. This development would potentially make it easier to preserve tax losses of a target company in a share sale for use by the purchaser post-completion.

[383] An income tax consolidation regime exists for companies which are 100% commonly owned and meet residence and other requirements. The broad effect of the consolidation rules is to treat the companies in the group as a single company for income tax purposes. Each member of a consolidated group is jointly and severally liable for income tax of the group, and this will be an important consideration when a share sale involves acquisition of target companies that are members of such a group. It is possible for the IRD, on request being made, to limit the joint and several liability of certain members of the consolidated group, effectively removing the liability of an exiting member. Provisions to accommodate this are typically included in a sale and purchase agreement for a share sale involving the acquisition of members of a consolidated group.

[384] The profits of an overseas incorporated subsidiary are not ordinarily imputed to its New Zealand shareholders under New Zealand's controlled foreign company (CFC) rules, provided that the subsidiary company either carries on an active business, or is resident, in Australia. Very broadly speaking, a company will carry on an active business for the purposes of the CFC rules where its passive income (e.g., interest, rent and royalties) does not exceed 5% of its gross income.

11.3.6 GST Consequences

[385] A share sale will typically be exempt from GST on the basis that the sale of shares is a supply of financial services (being the transfer of ownership of equity securities).

[386] An asset sale will be GST zero-rated where the assets include an interest in land (which could include freehold land or a lesser interest, such as a lease), provided that the seller and purchaser are each registered for GST, and the purchaser has the intention of using the land for the purposes of a taxable activity (and not as a place of residence for itself or an associate). Alternatively, zero-rating may be possible if the asset sale involves a supply of a taxable activity that is a going concern and the parties agree that zero-rating applies, although for most transactions an interest in land is necessary to be classified as a going concern.

11.3.7 Change of Control Consequences

[387] Any tax losses carried forward and any credits in the target company's ICA will be eliminated in a share sale transaction if, in the case of tax losses, 49% continuity of ownership and, in the case of imputation credits, 66% continuity of ownership, is not maintained. Calculation of the price for a target company should always therefore take into account any elimination of carried forward tax losses and imputation credits. It is usually possible to distribute any remaining imputation credits in a target company's ICA to its shareholders prior to the change in control, by way of either a dividend or a taxable bonus issue. A taxable bonus issue also increases the target's capital, which can be of benefit to a purchaser.

[388] As noted above, the proposed same or similar business test may allow tax losses to pass to a purchaser under a share sale, even where the 49% continuity of ownership test is not satisfied.

11.3.8 Employment Tax

[389] In an asset sale where employees of the seller's business accept employment with the purchaser, it is possible for the seller to obtain a deduction for annual leave and other employee entitlements provided for by the seller. This can be achieved provided that the seller and purchaser are not associated persons and the parties agree in writing (typically in the sale and purchase agreement relating to the transaction) that the purchaser assumes liability to pay the entitlements to the employee. *See* section 12.3.3 for more information on the process of transferring employees in an asset sale.

11.4 Deductibility of Financing Costs

[390] A New Zealand resident company is allowed a deduction for interest expenditure. By contrast, a non-resident company is not allowed a deduction, other than to the extent the interest relates to a business the company carries on through a New Zealand fixed establishment. In each case, the deductibility of interest is subject to the potential application of the thin capitalisation and transfer pricing rules, and anti-hybrid rules referred to below.

11.5 Thin Capitalisation

[391] New Zealand's thin capitalisation rules, in general terms, disallow certain interest deductions for a foreign-controlled New Zealand group where the group's debt to assets ratio (the *Debt Percentage*) exceeds 60% and that ratio is more than 110% of the Debt Percentage of a worldwide group of which the New Zealand group is a part.

11.6 Transfer Pricing

[392] New Zealand's transfer pricing rules require that cross-border transactions are priced on an arm's length basis. The transfer pricing rules are required to be applied consistently with the OECD's Transfer Pricing Guidelines. Deductibility of expenditure of a New Zealand party to a transfer pricing arrangement will be denied to the extent the expenditure exceeds an arm's length amount. Additionally, a New Zealand party to a transfer pricing arrangement will be deemed to have an amount of income to the extent the amount it derives falls short of an arm's length amount.

[393] Inbound loans between certain related parties may be subject to New Zealand's restricted transfer pricing rules. Those rules require the transfer pricing rules to be applied to qualifying loans on the basis that a deemed credit rating applies to the borrower and certain 'exotic' features of the relevant lending (e.g., subordination of the loan), if present, are ignored. A number of exceptions to the restricted transfer pricing rules apply, including a general exception where qualifying cross-border loans to which the borrower is a party are in aggregate less than NZD10 m.

11.7 Anti-hybrid Rules

[394] The Income Tax Act includes anti-hybrid rules intended to counteract tax advantages that might otherwise be obtained through a mismatch in the treatment of an arrangement or entity under New Zealand's tax rules and the tax rules of another jurisdiction. In structuring an M&A transaction involving investment into New Zealand it would be necessary to consider the potential application of the anti-hybrid rules to the acquisition structure and acquisition financing. In particular, it would be necessary to consider whether the transaction involves a deduction / non-inclusion outcome, a double deduction outcome or an 'imported hybrid mismatch' (in broad terms, a situation where a deduction in New Zealand is funded by an arrangement offshore that involves a hybrid mismatch).

11.8 Tax Treatment of Payments to and from Non-residents

11.8.1 Withholding Tax on Passive Income

[395] A company must deduct non-resident withholding tax (NRWT) from all non-resident passive income (NRPI) paid by it. Broadly put, NRPI comprises dividends, royalties and interest derived by non-residents who either do not carry on business in New Zealand through a fixed establishment or carry on business through a fixed establishment but do not meet certain other requirements.

[396] NRWT is imposed on the gross amount of the relevant taxpayer's NRPI. The rate of NRWT depends on the type of payment (i.e., dividend, interest or royalties), whether or not there is a DTA applicable and whether or not the non-resident deriving the payment is resident in the counterparty jurisdiction to the DTA, does not have a New Zealand permanent establishment and is entitled to benefit under the DTA.

[397] Under New Zealand's DTAs, interest and royalties will typically be subject to 10% NRWT, while dividends will be subject to either 15%, 5% or no NRWT depending on the terms of the relevant DTA and the circumstances of the non-resident.

[398] A 2% 'approved issuer levy' (AIL) can be paid effectively in lieu of NRWT on interest. However, AIL is not available where the relevant debt is 'related-party debt', meaning that AIL will not be available for debt between members of a group of companies. This regime is typically applied to interest payments on third-party debt (e.g., bank debt) provided by a non-resident lender to a resident borrower. Certain registrations are required to apply the AIL regime.

[399] The withholding tax treatment of dividends, interest and royalties is the same for both companies and individuals deriving such payments.

11.8.2 Non-resident Contractor's Tax

[400] A payment to a non-resident that performs services in New Zealand or provides personal property in New Zealand will usually attract a 15% withholding tax known as 'non-resident contractor's tax' (NRCT). A non-resident can apply for an exemption from NRCT in certain circumstances, including where it has full relief from tax under a DTA.

11.8.3 Other Relevant Considerations

[401] Interest and royalties derived by a New Zealand resident from overseas shareholders or other affiliates are taxable to the New Zealand resident. Dividends derived by a New Zealand company from a foreign subsidiary can be exempt from New Zealand tax, depending on the circumstances.

[402] Management or consultancy fees derived by a non-resident are not normally subject to withholding tax in New Zealand, unless the fees relate to the physical performance of services in New Zealand, in which case NRCT could apply.

[403] The deductibility of interest, royalties and management or consultancy fees can be affected by the transfer pricing rules described above. Additionally, deductibility of interest may be affected by the thin capitalisation rules and the anti-hybrid rules.

11.9 Incentives for Foreign Investment

[404] New Zealand does not currently have any special tax exemptions for corporate foreign investors such as tax sparing regimes or tax holidays.

[405] New Zealand does have some specific rules which may indirectly operate as an incentive for foreign investors, e.g., a zero rate of NRWT on dividends applies when such dividends are derived by certain non-portfolio, non-resident shareholders.

12 EMPLOYMENT

12.1 Overview of Employment Law

[406] Employment law in New Zealand is regulated by both legislation and common law. The main legislation governing employment relations is the Employment Relations Act 2000 (ERA).

12.1.1 Duty of Good Faith: ERA

[407] The concept of 'good faith' is the cornerstone of the ERA. The ERA states that all parties to an employment relationship (employers, employees and unions (if applicable)) owe a duty of good faith to the other party. The ERA describes the duty of good faith as requiring parties to an employment relationship not to mislead or deceive each other, to be active and constructive, and to be responsive and communicative in maintaining a productive employment relationship.

[408] If an employer is proposing to make a decision that will, or is likely to, have an 'adverse effect' on the continuation of an employee's employment, the employer must give the affected employee(s):

- access to information about the proposal (subject to certain requirements, including confidentiality); and
- an opportunity to comment before the decision is made.

[409] Examples of an 'adverse effect' include the termination of an employee's employment or a significant change to an employee's terms and conditions of employment, due to a restructure or sale of a business.

[410] In addition to the ERA, there are a number of other statutes which also regulate matters relating to the employment relationship.

12.1.2 Health and Safety at Work Act 2015

[411] The Health and Safety at Work Act 2015 (HSW Act) is the main statute regulating health and safety in the workplace. The HSW Act has significantly increased the responsibility and liability of directors and others in senior governance positions for health and safety breaches.

[412] The HSW Act requires a company or a business to ensure 'so far as is reasonably practicable', the health and safety of workers who work for the business. This requirement includes providing and maintaining a safe working environment and facilities, ensuring that a plant used by workers is safe for use, ensuring that risks to health and safety are eliminated or (where that is not reasonably practicable) minimised, and developing procedures for emergencies.

[413] In addition to the HSW Act duties owed by a company or business, officers of a business (including directors and others in senior governance positions) owe a 'due diligence' duty to take reasonable steps to ensure their business is compliant with its health and safety obligations under the HSW Act. This is a personal duty owed by each officer, and cannot be delegated, modified or transferred. Accordingly, an officer can be personally liable for a breach of this duty (rather than the company or business).

[414] Breaching the HSW Act is a criminal offence. Businesses and individuals (including directors and others in senior governance positions) can be subject to significant penalties, including fines and imprisonment for certain breaches.

[415] The most serious offence (reckless conduct) is subject to a maximum penalty for an individual of NZD600 000 or five years' imprisonment, or both, and for a body corporate, an NZD3 m fine. The courts also have other various powers, including the power to order enforceable undertakings (requiring businesses to carry out certain actions), and make adverse publicity orders.

12.1.3 Holidays Act 2003

[416] The Holidays Act 2003 (*Holidays Act*) sets out minimum entitlements in relation to holidays and other leave, including sick leave and bereavement leave. It is possible for the parties to agree on enhanced or additional entitlements to holidays or leave in the relevant individual employment agreement (IEA) or collective agreement (CEA).

[417] The Holidays Act provides four weeks' paid annual leave per year on the completion of twelve months' continuous service. The Holidays Act also sets out minimum entitlements for public holidays, sick leave, bereavement leave, and family violence leave.

[418] Risk of non-compliance with the Holidays Act is a common issue facing many New Zealand employers. This is due to the fact that the legislation is complex, there is uncertainty regarding the correct way to calculate holiday pay, and many employers rely on payroll systems which do not necessarily accurately calculate an employee's entitlements.

[419] Penalties for failure to comply with the Holidays Act are up to NZD20 000 (per breach), in addition to the relevant employing entity being liable to pay any leave entitlements determined to be outstanding for past and current employees for up to six years. Depending on the extent of non-compliance, these liabilities to pay leave entitlements can be significant.

[420] As a result of this common issue and potential significant liabilities, a purchaser needs to consider any potential Holidays Act non-compliance as part of any proposed acquisition. However, quantifying the potential liability for outstanding entitlements owing to employees will likely require a detailed audit to be undertaken by qualified accountants in order to identify any non-compliance, and this is unlikely to be achievable during the timetable for the proposed transaction. Accordingly, depending on the risk of non-compliance, the purchaser may need to consider including specific indemnities for any Holidays' Act liabilities in the sale agreement.

12.1.4 Other Key Employment Statutes

[421] Other legislation regulating employment relations matters include:

- *Minimum Wage Act*: The Minimum Wage Act sets out the mechanism for determining minimum wage rates for all employees aged 16 and over. The minimum wage rates are amended over time pursuant to Minimum Wage

Orders issued under the Minimum Wage Act. Employees must be paid at least the minimum hourly wage rate for every hour worked.
- *Human Rights Act*: A key objective of the Human Rights Act in respect of workplace relations is to provide protection from discrimination in the workplace.
- *Privacy Act*: The Privacy Act establishes rights and obligations in relation to the use of personal information about an individual that is held by an agency, which includes most employers. The Privacy Act sets out twelve information privacy principles which relate to the collection, storage, use and disclosure of personal information.
- *Accident Compensation Act*: The Accident Compensation Act sets out rights and obligations in relation to New Zealand's no-fault compensation scheme if someone is injured in an accident.
- *Parental Leave*: The Parental Leave and Employment Protection Act 1987 sets out minimum entitlements in relation to parental leave. Parental leave is comprised of several specific types of leave, including: primary carer leave, special leave, partner's leave, and extended leave. Each type of leave is subject to various eligibility requirements. Not all parental leave is paid in New Zealand.

12.2 Overview of Employment Relationships

12.2.1 Types of Employment

[422] There are three main types of employment in New Zealand: permanent, fixed-term and casual. These employment arrangements can be either full-time or part-time. The type of employment must be recorded in the IEA or CEA (as applicable):

- Permanent employment is the most common type of employment in New Zealand. Permanent employees are entitled to receive all employment-related benefits and rights provided under legislation.
- Fixed-term employees are only temporarily employed by an employer. These employees are employed either for a fixed period of time or for the duration of a specific project. An employer must have a genuine reason based on reasonable grounds for the fixed-term agreement. Fixed-term employees are entitled to the same statutory rights and benefits as a permanent employee except in relation to leave (unless the length of the fixed-term agreement means that they would qualify for such leave).
- Casual employees are employed on an 'as required' basis. In short, an employer is not required to provide the casual employee with work, and there is no obligation on the employee to accept work offered to them. Further, there is no expectation of ongoing employment after each work period. These employees are not entitled to the same statutory rights and benefits as permanent employees due to the unpredictable nature of casual work.

[423] There are a couple of other categories of worker in New Zealand:

- Self-employed workers are known as independent contractors in New Zealand. Independent contractors are not 'employees'. Accordingly, independent contractors are not entitled to receive employment-related benefits from any principal to whom they provide services.
- Agency workers perform work for an entity pursuant to a third-party business. Agency workers are often employed by the third-party business but not the entity to whom they provide services. However, these workers can bring a claim that they are 'jointly employed' by the agency and the entity to whom they provide services. These workers may also be able to join a 'controlling third party' to a personal grievance claim raised against their employer. The success of such a claim will depend on the facts of each case.

12.2.2 Types of Employment Agreements

[424] Pursuant to the ERA, an employee may enter into an IEA with an employer. The ERA sets out minimum requirements in relation to IEAs, including that all IEAs must be in writing. Before entering into an IEA, an employer must provide the prospective employee with a copy of the intended agreement, advise the employee that they are able to seek independent advice about the agreement and must give the prospective employee a reasonable opportunity to seek that advice.

[425] The alternative is for an employee to join a union. If the employee joins a union, that union may negotiate a CEA on behalf of its members. A CEA is only in force for a specific term and is renewed through collective bargaining. CEAs are generally limited to particular workplaces. However, some industries have multi-employer CEAs in place.

[426] New Zealand does not have any 'compulsory unionism' or works councils., the ERA does promote collective bargaining and provides a number of protections to trade unions. For example:

- Unions can only negotiate for a CEA (on behalf of its members) with employers. Employers and unions must negotiate for a CEA in good faith.
- Subject to a few limited exceptions, unions can access the workplace for union-related purposes (including for union business and recruitment of employees as union members) without the employer's consent if the employees are covered by a CEA or in bargaining towards a CEA.

[427] All employees have a limited right to strike or take other industrial action provided that it either relates to bargaining for a CEA or where the employee believes on reasonable grounds that industrial action is justified on the grounds of health and safety.

12.3 Employees in M&A

12.3.1 Consultation Obligations

[428] In accordance with the good faith provisions in the ERA, an employer is required to consult with affected employees and representatives (if any) about a proposal which could have an adverse effect on employees' ongoing employment. The obligation to consult applies in a number of circumstances, including a proposed asset sale, proposed redundancies, and proposed changes to employees' terms and conditions of employment (such as a change to pension schemes) if such proposed changes could have an 'adverse effect' on the employee's ongoing employment. However, the obligation to consult does not apply to a proposal to transfer shares of a company (provided that such transfer does not have an 'adverse effect' on the employee's ongoing employment).

[429] Consultation does not require obtaining affected employees' consent to the proposal. Rather, the requirement to consult includes providing affected employees with relevant information about the proposal and an opportunity to comment on the information before a decision is made. It is not possible to contract out of or derogate from these consultation obligations to the detriment of the employee. If an employer fails to comply with its consultation obligations:

- it may be liable for a financial penalty, of up to NZD20 000 per breach, where the breach of the consultation obligations is deliberate, serious and sustained or is intended to undermine the employment relationship;
- an employee/union may seek a compliance order from the Employment Relations Authority requiring the employer to consult prior to the proposal (such as an asset sale) going ahead. However, as noted above, consultation does not require obtaining affected employees' consent for the proposal. Accordingly, an employee/union cannot ultimately block the proposal from going ahead provided that the employer has complied with its consultation obligations (and these types of claims are therefore rare);
- the affected employees could claim that the failure to consult amounts to an unjustified disadvantage, and seek personal grievance remedies.

12.3.2 Vulnerable Employees

[430] The ERA provides for continuity of employment for certain categories of employees in the event of a business restructuring. In short, specified categories of employees may elect to transfer to the new employer where part or all of the business is sold or transferred, where the work carried out by the employee is contracted out or in, or where the contract for the work, previously undertaken by the affected employee as an employee of a contractor, is lost to a competitor. These employees include individuals in the cleaning industries and food catering services (among other limited categories) (*Vulnerable Employees*). In addition to complying with the consultation obligations as outlined in section 12.3.1 above, a seller must follow a specific process and timeframe in respect of Vulnerable Employees, including various notification obligations, prior to completion of the business transfer.

[431] Other affected employees (who are not Vulnerable Employees) only have limited protections in circumstances in which part or all of the business is sold or transferred. These employees do not have an automatic right to transfer to the purchaser. In accordance with the ERA, all IEAs must contain an 'employee protection provision'. This provision relates to the negotiation between the seller and the purchaser about the transfer of affected employees to the purchaser. Since there is no right for these affected employees to transfer, the onus is on the seller to do the best that it can in the context of the transaction to ensure that the employees are not at a disadvantage due to the sale of the business or assets.

12.3.3 Accrued Entitlements

[432] Where the shares of a company are being purchased, there is no change in the identity of the employer (it remains the same company). Accordingly, the company will continue to be responsible for its employees, and accrued employee entitlements, despite a change in the ultimate ownership of the company.

[433] Where the assets of a company are being purchased, accrued service-related entitlements do not transfer automatically with transferring employees as a matter of law (other than in relation to Vulnerable Employees). Unless otherwise agreed, liability for accrued service-related entitlements will remain with the current employer. However, in practice, it is common for the parties (i.e., the current employer, target and employee) to agree that accrued service-related entitlements 'transfer' to the new employer (so that the employees' leave balances essentially continue unchanged notwithstanding the change of employer).

12.4 Restraints of Trade

[434] In New Zealand, restraint of trade provisions is prima facie unenforceable. These provisions will only be upheld if it is reasonable to do so, having regard to the interests of the parties and the public. Restraints of trade in employment will only be upheld if the restraint of trade:

- is designed to protect the employer's legitimate proprietary interests (i.e., confidential information, trade connections or goodwill, or the stability of the employer's workforce); and
- does not extend further than is reasonably necessary to protect the employer's proprietary interests.

[435] Whether a restraint of trade is reasonable will be determined by such factors as the duration of the restraint, the geographical area that the restraint is intended to cover and the scope of activities restricted by the restraint. If the restraint is unenforceable because it is unreasonable, relief may be available under the Contract and Commercial Law Act 2017. That act provides a discretion for the courts to

modify, and then enforce, an unreasonable restraint of trade. However, the courts are reluctant to exercise the discretion to modify restraints which demonstrate a high degree of unreasonableness.

12.5 Pensions

12.5.1 No Compulsory Schemes

[436] New Zealand does not have any compulsory superannuation schemes. KiwiSaver is a voluntary superannuation scheme that all employers must enrol any new employees into (subject to a few limited exceptions). Currently, employees who participate in the scheme must contribute at least 3% of their gross salary or wages and employers must contribute 3% for each participating employee.

[437] However, many New Zealand employers facilitate workplace savings for their employees through one (or more) of the following vehicles:

- stand-alone superannuation scheme;
- multi-employer master trust; or
- KiwiSaver.

12.5.2 Stand-Alone Superannuation Scheme

[438] Traditionally, employers established their own stand-alone superannuation schemes, which have their own trust deed, trustees, and administration and investment managers. However, these schemes have significantly declined in number with multi-employer master trusts and KiwiSaver taking precedence.

[439] Stand-alone superannuation schemes typically operate on a defined contribution or defined benefit basis. There has been a trend away from defined benefit schemes and there are a few hybrid schemes in existence.

[440] If a scheme is funded on a defined contribution basis, benefits are based on contributions made by and in respect of a member, accumulated with interest.

[441] If a scheme is funded on a defined benefit basis, employers are required to contribute to the scheme such amount as is required to provide for the benefits of the scheme (typically determined by the employer with actuarial input). This means that the contributions required by the employer are not fixed and can fluctuate depending on the financial position of the scheme, and there is scope for the scheme to be underfunded or overfunded. For this reason, schemes funded on a defined benefit basis are typically the most problematic type of superannuation scheme to deal with in a transaction.

[442] The implications of an asset or share sale on a stand-alone scheme will depend on the governing documentation for the scheme. In an asset sale, the affected employees may no longer be entitled to participate in the scheme, and the purchaser may be required to offer them membership of an equivalent scheme or consider other compensation options. In a share sale, the purchaser may automatically inherit the scheme or the position may be the same as is generally the case for an asset sale. The purchaser will need to carefully review these arrangements as part of its due diligence.

12.5.3 Multi-Employer Master Trust

[443] A master trust is an umbrella superannuation scheme operated by a financial services company under which any number of unrelated employers can participate, while still allowing each employer to tailor the rules of the scheme for the needs of their own employees. It is an easy and simple alternative to an employer setting up their own stand-alone scheme. Master trusts typically operate on a defined contribution basis.

[444] As with stand-alone schemes, the implications of an asset or share sale on a stand-alone scheme will depend on the governing documentation for the scheme.

12.5.4 KiwiSaver

[445] KiwiSaver is a government-initiated, voluntary retirement savings scheme (pursuant to the KiwiSaver Act 2006). Participation in KiwiSaver is not mandatory for employees.

[446] Employees who choose to participate in KiwiSaver can choose which KiwiSaver scheme to join. Employees who commence new employment are generally automatically enrolled in KiwiSaver, but can choose to opt out within a certain period. Employers may select a preferred KiwiSaver scheme that all employees who join KiwiSaver but who do not select their own KiwiSaver scheme will be allocated to. If no choice is made by the employee or the employer as to which KiwiSaver scheme the employee joins, the employee will be assigned to one of the default KiwiSaver schemes approved by the Government

[447] Employees who choose to participate in KiwiSaver (or are automatically enrolled and do not opt out) must generally contribute a minimum of 3% of their gross salary or wages to their KiwiSaver scheme, subject to the ability to take a contributions holiday (which is a temporary cessation of KiwiSaver contributions).

[448] Subject to certain exemptions, employers are generally required to make minimum contributions of 3% of the relevant employee's gross salary or wages. Employers may choose to make employer contributions to employees' KiwiSaver accounts over and above the compulsory employer contributions

[449] KiwiSaver schemes are largely offered by fund managers rather than established by employers. Accordingly, in the context of an asset or share sale, generally the affected employees who are already members of a KiwiSaver scheme will remain members of the scheme, and the purchaser will be liable to make any applicable employer contributions to the scheme. In the context of an asset sale, the purchaser will generally need to give notice to the Commissioner of Inland Revenue to prevent the automatic enrolment in KiwiSaver of those transferring employees that are not already members of KiwiSaver.

12.6 Accident Compensation Scheme

[450] New Zealand has a 'no-fault' accident compensation scheme. The scheme provides financial assistance for medical expenses and loss of earnings to citizens, residents and temporary visitors who have suffered personal injuries for no-fault accidental injuries. In some situations, the scheme also provides compensation to individuals who suffer 'no-fault' accidental injuries. In return, the injured person is prevented from suing to recover damages for the accidental injury. There are now only limited circumstances in which an individual can sue for exemplary or punitive damages arising out of the accidental injury.

[451] The scheme is funded by levies paid by all employers, self-employed persons and employees, with additional funding being provided by the Government.

12.7 Immigration

[452] All employees must be legally eligible to work in New Zealand. An employee will be eligible to work if they are a citizen, have residency, or a work visa issued by Immigration New Zealand. It is an offence for an employer to employ an employee who is not legally eligible to work in New Zealand. As a general rule, work visas are likely to be granted if the prospective employee has the required skills and experience New Zealand needs and there are no locals available to do the work.

12.8 Other

12.8.1 Management Representation

[453] Employees are not entitled to management representation (i.e., to one or more seats on company boards) in New Zealand.

12.8.2 Redundancy

[454] There is no statutory right for an employee to be paid redundancy compensation in New Zealand. An employee is only entitled to a redundancy payment from their employer if this is provided for in their IEA or CEA.

12.8.3 Termination of Employment

[455] In New Zealand, an employee can resign from their employment by giving notice (as set out in their IEA or CEA (as applicable)). Unless an employee has a

valid statutory ninety-day trial period provision in their IEA or CEA (as applicable) an employer must have 'good cause' for terminating an employment relationship as well as give notice in accordance with the IEA or CEA (as applicable). However, notice is not required if an employer is terminating an employee's employment for serious misconduct. An employer must follow a full and fair process prior to terminating an employee's employment. The process an employer must follow varies depending on the reason for the termination.

12.8.4 Unjustified Dismissal

[456] An employee has a right to bring a personal grievance claim if they consider their termination was unjustified, or they consider they have been subject to an unjustified disadvantage.

[457] If a dismissal is found to be both substantively and procedurally unjustified, an employee may potentially receive reimbursement of wages (the starting presumption being three months' remuneration); compensation for humiliation, loss of dignity and injury to feelings; and a contribution towards legal costs (based on a daily tariff rate). In addition, an employee may potentially be reinstated to their previous position.

13 DISPUTE RESOLUTION

13.1 Contractual Disputes

13.1.1 Overview

[458] Contractual disputes arising under New Zealand law may be determined by reference to common law, statute, or a combination thereof. Matters relating to the validity and enforceability of common contractual clauses, such as restrictive covenants, are mostly determined under the common law. Other matters are subject to the provisions of the Contract and Commercial Law Act 2017, which includes provisions governing contractual mistakes, remedies, frustration, and illegal contracts.

13.1.2 Validity and Enforceability

[459] Turning first to questions of validity and enforceability, sophisticated, commercial parties should expect relatively few obstacles to enforcement of common contractual provisions in mergers and acquisitions (subject to the practical constraints noted in section 13.2 below). Caution is, however, required when drafting restraint of trade clauses that restrict individuals from carrying on a business, trade or profession, whether in New Zealand or overseas (*see* section 5.3).

13.1.3 Remedies

[460] The primary remedy in New Zealand for breach of contract is an action for damages. Damages are intended to place the innocent party in the position it would have been in, but for the breach. These are commonly calculated on the basis of reliance (compensation for steps taken by the innocent party in reliance on the contract) or expectation (compensation placing the innocent party in the position it would have been in, had the contract been performed).

[461] While damages, as noted above, are the primary remedy for breach of contract, there are some cases where an innocent party may sue for specific performance of the contract, that is, forcing the party in breach to comply with its contractual obligations. Specific performance will not be ordered if the innocent party has an alternative, adequate remedy available at law. For this reason, specific performance is rarely ordered except in relation to contracts involving interests in land. A court may also make an injunction, requiring a party in breach (or intending to breach) to refrain from taking specified actions or, if the breach has already occurred, requiring the breaching party to take positive steps to reverse the actions taken in breach.

[462] Breach of contract may also entitle the innocent party to cancel the contract in certain circumstances. Under the Contract and Commercial Law Act, a party to a contract may cancel it if the party has been induced to enter into the contract by a misrepresentation of substantial significance, or if there has been or will be a breach of an essential term of the contract. These rights may be modified if there is a particular contractual provision dealing with the consequences of breach or misrepresentation. It is common practice in sale agreements for the parties to specify the particular circumstances where a party can cancel the agreement. These are usually for failure to satisfy a condition precedent or to perform the parties' obligations on completion of the sale. It is not common for a breach of warranties or representations to give rise to a right to cancel the sale agreement.

[463] Contractual provisions stipulating consequences for breach of contract are generally enforceable, provided that the clause does not amount to an unenforceable penalty. New Zealand courts have recently followed UK authority in holding that a clause will not amount to an unenforceable penalty so long as it protects a legitimate interest in the performance of the contract, and provided that the consequences of breach are not out of all proportion to the legitimate interest in question.

13.2 Governing Law

13.2.1 Jurisdiction and Choice of Law

[464] Under New Zealand law, the question of jurisdiction is determined by reference to service. In the case of a company (including any foreign body corporate), jurisdiction may be established by the service of documents commencing proceedings on the corporation in New Zealand in accordance with the relevant provisions of the High Court Rules 2016 and the Companies Act. This principle extends to service properly effected outside of New Zealand in defined circumstances, notably in respect of proceedings in contract where the contract in question was made or performed in New Zealand or was, by its terms or by implication, to be governed by New Zealand law.

[465] A New Zealand court that has jurisdiction to hear and determine a proceeding may nevertheless decline to do so if there is another court with jurisdiction to hear the matter that is a more suitable forum for resolution of the dispute (*forum conveniens*). Where the parties to a contract have agreed to submit exclusively to a foreign jurisdiction or forum, the onus is on the applicant to demonstrate that New Zealand is *forum conveniens* – for example, because a foreign court could not grant the relief sought. Where the parties have agreed to exclusive New Zealand jurisdiction, however, this will not automatically mean that New Zealand is *forum conveniens* if the dispute could be more appropriately resolved in another forum. Non-exclusive jurisdiction clauses are of little relevance to determination of the *forum conveniens*.

[466] If it is determined that the New Zealand courts have jurisdiction and are an appropriate forum in which to hear and determine proceedings, a further question arises as to the law that should be applied. In the case of a contractual dispute, this will be the 'proper law' of the contract. Where the parties to a contract have stipulated a choice as to governing law, this will generally be the proper law unless there are strong public policy reasons to the contrary. In other cases, the court will determine the proper law from the terms of the contract and the surrounding circumstances. Where the contract is to be performed entirely in one country, this will be a highly influential factor in determining the proper law.

13.2.2 Cross-Border Enforceability

[467] The recognition and enforceability of foreign judgments in New Zealand are determined by a combination of statute and common law. Different statutory provisions apply, based on the origin of the foreign judgment:

(i) as between New Zealand and Australia, the Trans-Tasman Agreement provides for the mutual recognition and enforcement of specified judgments in New Zealand, including most final and conclusive judgments of Australian courts in civil matters;
(ii) the Reciprocal Enforcement of Judgments Act 1934 provides for the recognition and enforcement in New Zealand of money judgments given in the senior courts of specified foreign countries, including the UK and France; and
(iii) subject to the Reciprocal Enforcement of Judgments Act, money judgments issued by any court of a Commonwealth country may be enforced under the Senior Courts Act 2016, provided that the judgment is of a kind enforceable at common law.

[468] Foreign judgments that are not enforceable in New Zealand under statute may be enforceable at common law on the basis that these represent an outstanding debt owed by the judgment debtor to the judgment creditor. Full satisfaction of the foreign judgment is a complete defence to the attempted enforcement of a foreign judgment under common law and bars any further proceedings in New Zealand in respect of the judgment.

[469] The enforceability of a New Zealand judgment in a foreign jurisdiction is generally a matter to be determined in accordance with the laws of that jurisdiction. However, as noted above, the Trans-Tasman Agreement provides for the mutual recognition and enforcement of specified New Zealand judgments in Australia, including final and conclusive judgments of New Zealand courts in civil matters.

13.3 Court Proceedings

[470] The New Zealand court system is relatively streamlined, compared with many countries. There are four courts of general jurisdiction: the District Court, High Court, Court of Appeal and Supreme Court. These are supplemented by a small number of specialist tribunals, such as the Environment Court and Employment Court. The court system is robust, with a strong emphasis on judicial independence. Parties can expect that proceedings will be determined fairly and impartially on the merits, without regard to nationality, residence or choice of business vehicle (except, of course, in so far as such matters are legally relevant). Judges are subject to independent oversight by the Judicial Conduct Commissioner; however instances of misconduct are extremely rare.

[471] Commercial cases are ordinarily commenced in the High Court at first instance, with a right of appeal to the Court of Appeal and, with leave, the Supreme Court. There is no specialist commercial court in New Zealand; however, complex and/or high-value commercial cases may be allocated to a member of the High Court's commercial panel, comprising High Court judges with particular expertise in commercial law. The vast majority of proceedings involving commercial parties are resolved by judge-alone trial.

[472] The High Court, as both a Court of First Instance and an appellate court from some lower courts and tribunals, has a busy caseload. It can therefore vary widely in terms of the time it takes to bring a proceeding from initial filing through to delivery of the substantive judgment. There is an element of flexibility in scheduling, and urgent matters are often dealt with relatively expeditiously. In some cases, however, it may be a year or more before a substantive hearing can be scheduled, particularly if there are disputes regarding interlocutory matters. The majority of judgments are delivered within three months of the hearing date, although delays can be possible in complex cases.

13.4 Mediation

[473] Mediation is a voluntary process which involves the appointment of a third-party mediator to facilitate discussion and resolution of disputes. Mediation is not a legal proceeding and parties do not need to be legally represented in order to participate (although legal representation is common in the context of commercial disputes). Discussions and disclosures made during the mediation process are generally confidential, except to the extent that these reveal physical danger to any person or serious criminality. Mediation is without prejudice to the dispute which means that what was said at the mediation may not be revealed in a subsequent arbitration or court proceeding.

[474] Contractual clauses requiring mediation in the event of a dispute remain uncommon and parties are more inclined to agree to mediation if and when there is shared desire to try and resolve the dispute outside of a binding dispute resolution process (i.e., outside of arbitration, adjudication or court).

13.5 Arbitration

[475] Arbitration combines aspects of both mediation and litigation. It is a voluntary process agreed to by the parties either in the commercial contract itself or separately in an agreement to arbitrate (which may be made either before or after a dispute has arisen). An arbitration involves appointment of an independent third party with the power to render a binding decision regarding the dispute that is enforceable at law.

[476] Arbitration is a popular mechanism for dispute resolution in the commercial context in New Zealand, both in the cross-border and, increasingly, the domestic contexts. New Zealand is a party to the Convention on the Recognition and Enforcement of Foreign Arbitral Awards, more commonly known as the New York Convention.

[477] Arbitration is governed in New Zealand by the Arbitration Act 1996 (the *Arbitration Act*). The Arbitration Act applies primarily in respect of arbitrations conducted in New Zealand but makes provision for matters arising in relation to arbitrations and awards outside New Zealand, in particular, recognition and enforcement of arbitral awards. Generally, where there is an arbitration agreement in place between disputing parties, New Zealand courts will require those parties to resolve their differences via arbitration rather than court proceedings unless the agreement is null and void, inoperative or incapable of being performed. A court may, if necessary, make interim orders pending the outcome of arbitral proceedings. Otherwise, court involvement is limited, reflecting the purpose of arbitration.

[478] The High Court may set aside an arbitral award on the application of a party but only in very limited circumstances – for example, where a party to the arbitration agreement was unable to present its case or where the subject matter of the dispute is not capable of settlement by arbitration under New Zealand law.

14 OTHER RELEVANT LAWS

14.1 Property

14.1.1 Common Types of Land in New Zealand

[479] Most land in New Zealand is registered with the New Zealand land registry maintained by LINZ. Title to land registered at LINZ is guaranteed by the Crown, and the registry is publicly searchable. The two main types of land in New Zealand are freehold (or fee simple) land and leasehold land.

[480] An owner of freehold land is regarded as enjoying the highest level of property ownership in New Zealand, as a freehold title confers ownership without any limitation as to term. A freehold title is issued by LINZ, with the owner of the land being noted as 'registered owner' of the 'record of title' for the land.

[481] A leasehold interest in land is granted by the owner of the freehold title (the lessor) to the owner of the leasehold title (the lessee) by way of a lease which is limited as to its term. The lessee enjoys exclusive possession and quiet enjoyment of the land, subject to any conditions imposed under the lease (and any requirements under law or regulation). Although leasehold can be registered at LINZ, it is more common for leasehold land to be unregistered in New Zealand (as registration is not a statutory requirement), particularly for a shorter term, occupational leases.

[482] Other less common forms of property ownership in New Zealand include:

- Māori land, which is held under the Te Ture Whenua Māori Act 1993 which recognises the traditional Māori practice of joint customary ownership (as opposed to individual ownership) of land. Māori land is administered by the Māori Land Court, as well as LINZ;
- unit titles, which grant ownership of part of a development (usually apartments); and
- cross leases, which were commonly used in the latter half of the twentieth century as a means to effectively circumvent rules regarding subdivision of land, but which are rarely used in modern developments.

14.1.2 Overview of Key Property Legislation

[483] The key laws governing property in New Zealand include:

(i) the Property Law Act 2007 (*Property Law Act*), which is wide-ranging and governs a broad range of property interests and transactions, and includes laws relating to the assignment or transfer of interests in land, leases, including terms which are implied into leases in New Zealand and mortgages and the exercise by mortgagees of any power of sale they may have over mortgaged land;

(ii) the Land Transfer Act 2017, which governs the registration of land ownership in New Zealand;
(iii) the Building Act 2004 (*Building Act*), which sets the standards and procedures for the building or alteration of buildings and other structures in New Zealand. It allows territorial authorities, such as local councils, to regulate the building activity within their district; and
(iv) the Resource Management Act 1991 (RMA), which regulates the use of land in New Zealand. Refer to section 14.2 below for further information in relation to the RMA.

14.1.3 Transfer of Property Interests

[484] The transfer of freehold interests in land occurs via the LINZ database. Most freehold land is now conveyed electronically via the LINZ 'e-dealing' system, which involves lawyers for both the transferor and the transferee certifying the transfer (on the instructions of their respective clients). In most cases, the transfer of a freehold title is registered with LINZ instantaneously.

[485] The transfer of a registered leasehold interest also occurs via the LINZ database and follows the same process as the transfer of a freehold interest. Unregistered leasehold interests however are not transferred via the LINZ database and are instead assigned via written documentation (commonly a deed of assignment of lease, executed by the lessor, the lessee and the assignee). Whether the lease is registered or unregistered, the lessee is typically required to satisfy certain conditions contained in the lease before the assignment is permitted. These are outlined in more detail below.

Asset Sales

[486] In an asset sale, the particular freehold or leasehold interests that are to be transferred or assigned to the purchaser will be outlined in the asset sale agreement, including the process and responsibility for transferring title to freehold and registered leasehold land.

[487] Leases in New Zealand typically prohibit assignment without the prior written consent of the lessor, which may not be unreasonably withheld or delayed provided that certain pre-conditions set out in the lease are met. These might include that the:

- lessor is satisfied that the assignee is respectable, responsible and has the financial resources to meet its commitments under the lease;
- assignor has paid all rent and other moneys owing under the lease, and is not in breach of the lease; and
- assignee provides a parent company guarantee (or other suitable security, such as a bank guarantee).

[488] However, under the Property Law Act (and notwithstanding the terms of the lease), a lessor may not enforce any such conditions unless reasonable in the circumstances.

[489] The ongoing liability of assignors is another important consideration. Under the Property Law Act, an assignor of a lease remains liable for the performance of the lessee's obligations under the lease by the assignee during the then current lease term, unless a release of liability is obtained from the lessor.

Share Sales

[490] In a share sale, the company being sold will continue to hold any property interests after completion, without any transfer of property interests required. However, a change of control of the lessee company may be deemed to be an assignment of many leases in New Zealand, triggering the requirement for lessor consent. This may depend on where the change of control takes place in the transaction – whether it be in the shares of the lessee entity itself, its immediate shareholder or its ultimate parent company.

14.1.4 Seismic Strength Issues

[491] Consideration of the seismic rating of any buildings forming part of any property is important, especially if the property is located in the areas of New Zealand classed as medium or high-risk seismic areas. Under the Building Act, owners of 'earthquake-prone' buildings (measured by reference to the applicable building standards) must strengthen those buildings within the timeframes set out in the Building Act, which vary depending on the location, type and use of buildings involved.

[492] Although this is usually of particular concern to purchasers who will be acquiring freehold properties and therefore responsible for the costs of undertaking such seismic strengthening work, this can also be relevant for lessees. Under the HSW Act, a lessee who is an employer must ensure, so far as is reasonably practicable, the health and safety of their workers and any visitors to their premises. Where a lessee's premises are of such low seismic strength that they present a danger to their staff and visitors, then lessees may be faced with little option but to vacate the premises. Depending on the terms of the relevant lease, the lessee may be required to continue paying rent despite having vacated the premises. In addition, under the terms of some leases, the lessee may be liable for some or all of the costs of the seismic strengthening work, or the lessor may be able to increase the rent if it is required at law to undertake such works.

14.2 Environmental

14.2.1 Overview of the RMA 1991

[493] The RMA is the key environmental legislation in New Zealand. Under the provisions of the RMA, district and regional councils are required to prepare and administer plans to regulate the effects of activities on the environment.

[494] District councils control the effects of the use, development and protection of land. District plans usually regulate the use of land through the implementation of zones. The rules for a particular zone will determine whether an activity requires a resource consent under the RMA.

[495] Regional councils' responsibilities include the allocation of water, and discharges of contaminants to air, water and land where it may enter water. Regional plans include rules setting levels or standards for taking water, and discharges of a contaminant.

14.2.2 Resource Consents

[496] If a proposed activity does not comply with the provisions of the relevant district or regional plan then a resource consent will be required. Resource consents authorise the particular activity for which consent was sought, and are subject to conditions which must be complied with by any new owner / operator.

[497] The resource consent process requires an application to be lodged with the relevant council, and can involve consultation with affected parties, limited or public notification, a council hearing and decision, and, an appeal to the Environment Court (as a hearing de novo) or higher courts (on points of law only).

[498] Once granted, a resource consent usually contains conditions about the way the activity can be carried out, which aim to minimise the negative environmental effects of the activity. These can include requirements to rehabilitate the land upon completion of the activity for which consent is granted, and the imposition of covenants or financial security arrangements (bonds) in respect of the performance of such condition (or any other condition), which may be registered against the title to the land. Consent conditions may also require the consent holder to undertake monitoring or management of the site in order to avoid, remedy or mitigate adverse effects.

14.2.3 Contamination

[499] Regional councils are required to keep a register of potentially contaminated land within their respective regions. Councils identify sites to be included on the register where the land is known to be contaminated, or an activity on the Hazardous Activities and Industries List (HAIL) has occurred, or does occur, on the property. The HAIL indicates that such activities and industries are more likely to use or store hazardous substances and therefore there is a greater probability of site contamination occurring compared to other uses or activities. Inclusion of a property on the Register does not mean that a site is contaminated, and conversely a property that does not appear on the Register does not guarantee such a site will not be contaminated.

[500] In the absence of obtaining the necessary consent under the RMA for the discharge of contaminants, action can be taken under the RMA for contamination that occurred after 1991 (as the RMA is not retrospective in effect). Under the RMA, the polluter, owner and/or occupier of land on which contaminants have been unlawfully discharged may be subject to enforcement action on a strict liability basis and there is no defence for 'innocent owners'. If the original polluter is no longer in existence or is unable to be identified or located, then the current owner would be likely to be expected to undertake remediation (and could recover the costs of that exercise from the original polluter if they can be identified). For contamination caused prior to 1991, action can be brought against the polluter under the common law (by way of an action in tort for nuisance and/or negligence).

14.2.4 Liability and Enforcement

[501] Enforcement or prosecution proceedings under the RMA can be initiated for failure to comply with the provisions of the RMA, resource consents, district or regional plan rules, or for environmental incidents. Where a company is convicted of an offence under the RMA, the directors and managers will also be liable if it is established that the offence took place with such person's authority, consent or permission, or that he/she knew or could reasonably be expected to have known of the offence and failed to take all reasonable steps to stop it. In certain circumstances, companies within a corporate group may also be liable for the offence, for example, if a subsidiary company was acting as an agent for a parent company and if the directors or any person involved in the management of the parent company knew, or could reasonably be expected to have known, that the offence was to be, or was being, committed.

14.2.5 Publicly Available Information

[502] In New Zealand, most district and regional councils do not have searchable online information to find resource consent, contamination and enforcement history relating to particular properties. As a result, it is necessary to make formal requests to the councils for copies of this information. Councils have twenty working days to respond to official information requests. One challenge in the due diligence process can therefore be obtaining the necessary information within the timeframes required for the transaction.

[503] In addition to the HAIL register, district councils prepare Land Information Memorandum (known as LIM Reports) on properties. The LIM Reports may identify if the property is subject to geotechnical issues, flooding risks, archaeological sites, and in wind zones. These issues may mean the property is not suitable for further development, may require additional technical assessment or could have increased costs (or require increased time) associated with future development.

14.2.6 Impact of Sale on Environmental Liabilities

[504] The main implications of the nature of a transaction (share sale versus asset sale) from a resource management perspective, is how environmental liabilities are addressed and whether resource consents need to be transferred.

[505] A share sale will result in the purchaser acquiring the shares in the company which has the environmental liabilities, that is, any environmental liabilities will automatically transfer (unless there are contractual limitations and warranties and/or indemnities).

[506] In an asset sale, environmental liabilities may be passed with the asset to the purchaser as 'innocent new owners' can still be subject to enforcement action (in addition to the original polluter if they are still in existence), or excluded by contract.

[507] Another implication is resource consents for activities under a regional plan such as water and discharge permits are held by a consent holder and so need to be transferred to a new owner / operator in an asset sale by giving written notice to the regional council. Land use consents do not usually need to be transferred as they typically run with the land.

14.3 Intellectual Property

[508] IP rights in New Zealand can be broadly categorised into registered and unregistered rights.

14.3.1 Registrable IP

[509] In New Zealand, the following forms of IP are registrable: trademarks, patents, designs, geographical indications, plant varieties and domain names. A registration is a particularly effective tool for enforcing IP rights against third parties and is generally relatively simple and inexpensive to obtain. It is therefore advisable to seek registration where possible.

[510] The registration of trademarks, patents, designs, geographical indications, and plant varieties is administered by the Intellectual Property Office of New Zealand (IPONZ), the central IP office operated by the New Zealand Government.

[511] Key IP registered with IPONZ include:

- *Trademarks*: The holder of a registered mark in New Zealand has the exclusive right to use that mark in relation to the registered goods and/or services. A trademark registration is renewable indefinitely, in ten-year intervals.
- *Patents*: A registered patent can grant the owner the exclusive right to exclude others from dealing with the invention under the patent in New Zealand, whether it be a particular product or process. A patent has a maximum term of twenty years.
- *Designs*: A registered design grants rights in the particular appearance of an article of manufacture, such as shape, configuration, pattern or ornament. The article must be new or original, have a degree of eye-appeal and be more than merely functional. A registration can last up to fifteen years.

[512] The New Zealand Domain Name Commission has jurisdiction over the handling of '.nz' domain names, and there are a number of private registrars through which these can be acquired and managed. Domain names are an anomalous form of IP registration. Like a company name, the ownership of a domain name does not in itself confer use rights in the name; these are conferred through a trademark registration or use. However, the use of a domain name can assist in the accrual of unregistered trademark rights in that name and a domain name registration can comprise part of the valuable assets of a business.

14.3.2 Unregistered IP

[513] In addition to registered rights, there is a suite of unregistered rights which are recognised in New Zealand and which provide alternative and supplementary IP protections. These include trademark rights, copyright, know-how, confidential information, and trade secrets. In particular:

- *Unregistered trademark rights:* these rights accrue by virtue of the goodwill and reputation established in a particular mark (registered or otherwise) in New Zealand through use. These rights can form the basis of civil action to prevent the use and registration of the identical or confusingly similar mark.
- *Copyright*: copyright automatically arises upon the creation of an original work (its eligibility as defined under the Copyright Act 1994). The author of a work will be the first owner of its copyright unless the work was created under a commissioning or employment arrangement, in which case the commissioning party or employer will own the copyright, or there is an agreement to the contrary. The owner has the exclusive authority (subject to certain qualifications) to make and deal with copies of that work. For works such as literary and musical works, the duration of copyright is fifty years from the death of the author.

14.3.3 Creation of IP

[514] Subject to any agreement to the contrary, where:

- an employee during the course of employment creates any literary, dramatic, musical or artistic work, the copyright in this work will be owned by the employer; or
- a person commissions and pays for the creation of certain works such as the making of a computer programme, the person who commissions and pays for that work will own that work.

[515] These 'rules' have been codified in the Copyright Act 1994. However, at common law, the presumption of ownership by an employer or the person who commissions and pays for works applies more broadly and includes the creation of inventions.

[516] Notwithstanding the above, it is generally a best practice wherever possible for parties to agree in advance on the question of ownership with respect to any IP that may be created and record such agreement in writing. If a party is acquiring IP as part of an M&A transaction, the relevant agreements should be reviewed to confirm who owns the relevant IP, particularly if that IP is unregistered.

14.3.4 Transfer of IP

[517] Where a transaction is structured as a share sale, all IP owned and held by the target company will transfer on sale (subject to any agreement to the contrary) including any liabilities associated with that IP. To ensure that the purchaser retains all IP rights that are material and/or necessary for the continued operation of the business, it is important for the purchaser to carry out due diligence to confirm that all such IP assets are owned or validly licensed for use by the target company, and for any issues (in particular with respect to infringement of IP) and inconsistencies to be resolved prior to completion.

[518] Under an asset sale structure, only the IP, whether registered or unregistered, specifically transferred either as part of the sale agreement or separate deed of assignment will be sold to the purchaser.

[519] In respect of registered IP or domain names, any change in ownership should also be reflected by updating the relevant public register. Recordals of changes in ownership of registered patents, trademarks and designs are administered by IPONZ, which will update the ownership details upon receipt of an application for recordal together with documentation evidencing the change of title (such as an assignment agreement). For domain name registrations, the process of updating such details and transferring control is particular to the registry with which the domain name is registered and will usually require the completion of a form by both the seller and purchaser.

14.4 Consumer Protection Laws

14.4.1 Overview

[520] The Consumer Guarantees Act 1993 (*Consumer Guarantees Act*) and the Fair Trading Act 1986 (*Fair Trading Act*) are New Zealand's primary consumer protection legislation. Together, they aim to protect the interests of consumers, enable businesses to compete effectively and facilitate a trading environment in New Zealand where consumers and businesses can participate confidently.

14.2.2 Consumer Guarantees Act

[521] The Consumer Guarantees Act sets out statutory guarantees relating to goods and services that are ordinarily acquired for personal, domestic or household use or consumption. If the goods or services fail to comply with a guarantee, the Consumer Guarantees Act provides statutory rights and remedies.

[522] In respect of goods, the guarantees set out in the Consumer Guarantees Act relate to title (ownership), time of delivery, acceptable quality, fitness for a particular purpose, compliance with description or sample, price (if unspecified), repairs and spare parts, and express guarantees. In respect of services, the Consumer Guarantees Act provides guarantees as to reasonable care and skill, fitness for purpose, time of completion and price.

[523] The Consumer Guarantees Act provides rights and remedies against both suppliers and manufacturers where goods or services fall short of the guarantees in the Consumer Guarantees Act. Different rights and remedies will arise where the failure can be remedied; the failure cannot be remedied, or the failure is substantial; or there is consequential loss due to a breach of a guarantee. For example, under the Consumer Guarantees Act, where goods are not of acceptable quality or fit for their particular purpose, consumers are entitled to require the goods to be repaired or replaced (at the supplier's election). Where there is a defect which cannot be remedied or is of a substantial character, the consumer may reject the goods and seek a replacement or refund.

14.4.3 Fair Trading Act

[524] The Fair Trading Act aims to promote fair competition and consumer welfare by prohibiting unfair conduct, promoting product safety and ensuring consumers are provided with accurate information in relation to goods and services. In particular, the Fair Trading Act prohibits misleading and deceptive conduct, unsubstantiated, misleading or false representations, unfair practices and the use of unfair contract terms in standard form consumer contracts.

[525] The Fair Trading Act also sets out mandatory disclosure and cancellation requirements for extended warranty agreements and all agreements for consumer goods or services that are entered into as a result of an 'uninvited direct sale' (e.g., through telemarketing sales). It also provides for the establishment of consumer information standards and product and service safety standards.

[526] The Fair Trading Act applies to anyone 'in trade', including overseas businesses carrying on business within New Zealand. The Fair Trading Act may also apply to conduct performed overseas if it relates to the supply of goods or services, or granting of interests in land, within New Zealand.

[527] The Fair Trading Act contains both civil and criminal enforcement provisions. A consumer can bring a civil proceeding against a business. Alternatively, the Commerce Commission can bring proceedings against a business for breaches of the Fair Trading Act. Commercial entities can be liable to a fine of up to NZD600 000, and individuals to a fine of up to NZD200 000 (per offence). The courts also have powers to award damages, issue infringement notices, void contracts, vary contracts, issue injunctions to prevent conduct recurring, order the refund of money or the return of goods, order that corrective statements be published and declare that unfair terms in standard form consumer contracts are unenforceable.

[528] The Ministry of Business, Innovation and Employment is currently considering whether there is a need for additional protection for businesses against unfair commercial practices, and in particular, unfair contract terms in business-to-business transactions. At the time of writing, this reform is at an early consultation stage.

14.4.4 Contracting out of Consumer Protection Legislation

[529] As a general rule, businesses cannot contract out of the Consumer Guarantees Act or Fair Trading Act when supplying goods and services to consumers. A limited exception allows contracting out of the Consumer Guarantees Act and certain provisions of the Fair Trading Act[18] in 'business-to-business' agreements. In particular, where:

(i) all parties agree to contracting out in a written agreement;
(ii) all parties to the agreement are in trade;
(iii) the goods and/or services are supplied and acquired in trade; and
(iv) it is fair and reasonable that the parties are bound by such an agreement.

[530] Courts will judge what is 'fair and reasonable' based on a range of factors, including whether there is equality in bargaining power, the conduct of the parties, access to legal advice and the ability to negotiate. In all other circumstances, it is an offence to try to contract out of the Consumer Guarantees Act or Fair Trading Act.

14.5 Privacy and Data Protection

14.5.1 Privacy Act

[531] The Privacy Act 1993 is New Zealand's primary privacy and data protection legislation. It applies to every business and organisation (referred to as 'agencies' throughout the Privacy Act) in New Zealand that collects personal information about individuals, including employees and consumers (subject to very limited exceptions). The Privacy Act 1993 will be replaced by the Privacy Act 2020 when it comes into force on 1 December 2020 and the Privacy Act 2020 represents a long-awaited update to New Zealand's privacy laws. Except where expressly stated otherwise, the overview of the 'Privacy Act' in this section applies to both the Privacy Act 1993 and the Privacy Act 2020.

[532] The Privacy Act sets out twelve 'Information Privacy Principles' which provide substantive requirements in relation to dealing with personal information. These principles cover the collection, storage, use, access, correction and disclosure of personal information. The Privacy Act also governs individuals' rights to access and request correction of their personal information. Under the Privacy Act, every agency is required to appoint a Privacy Officer. Personal information is

[18] A business can contract out of ss 9, 12A, 13 and 14(1) of the Fair Trading Act.

defined as 'information about an identifiable individual'. Even if information does not directly identify a specific individual, if it can be linked with other information to identify a specific individual, then it will constitute personal information.

[533] The Privacy Commissioner can issue 'codes of practice' under the Privacy Act that modify the operation of the Privacy Act for specific industries, agencies, activities or types of personal information. There are currently six codes of practice, including codes that apply to credit reporters, telecommunications agencies and health agencies.[19]

[534] Some of the key changes of the Privacy Act 2020 include:

(i) mandatory reporting of privacy breaches;
(ii) applicability of the Privacy Act to overseas entities that are carrying on business in New Zealand;
(iii) strengthening of cross-border data flow protections;
(iv) new powers of the Privacy Commissioner, including to issue compliance notices and make binding decisions; and
(v) the introduction of new criminal offences.

[535] In relation to privacy breaches, the Privacy Act 2020 places obligations on agencies to report privacy breaches to the Privacy Commissioner and affected individual(s) where it is reasonable to believe the breach has caused or is likely to cause serious harm to affected individual(s).

[536] Under the Privacy Act 2020, for particular breaches, the Privacy Commissioner can commence criminal proceedings which can attract a fine of up to NZD10 000. The Human Rights Review Tribunal can award damages under the Privacy Act of up to NZD350 000.

[537] The Unsolicited Electronic Messages Act 2007 is also relevant to the use of personal information in New Zealand. The key purpose of the Unsolicited Electronic Messages Act 2007 is to prohibit the sending of unsolicited commercial electronic messages with a New Zealand link. 'Commercial electronic messages' are electronic messages (such as emails and text messages) that market or promote goods, services, land or a business or investment opportunity.

14.5.2 Transfer of Information

[538] In New Zealand, generally, the implementation of a share sale or asset sale will not give rise to particular privacy issues. The Privacy Act expressly permits personal information to be disclosed to a purchaser, without authorisation of the individuals concerned, where the agency that is transferring the personal information

[19] At the date of publication, the codes of practice issued are the Civil Defence National Emergencies (Information Sharing) Code 2013, Credit Reporting Privacy Code 2004, Health Information Privacy Code 1994, Justice Sector Unique Identifier Code 1998, Superannuation Schemes Unique Identifier Code 1995 and the Telecommunications Information Privacy Code 2003. The Privacy Commissioner is seeking submissions on the proposed repeal and replacement of these privacy codes of practice to align with the reforms in the Privacy Act 2020.

believes on reasonable grounds that the disclosure is 'necessary to facilitate the sale or other disposition of a business as a going concern'.

[539] In terms of transferring information:

(i) *Share sale*: where the shareholding of the target entity changes, the personal information is retained by the target entity. No new disclosure or transfer of personal information is likely to be required; and
(ii) *Asset sale*: in the context of an asset sale, if a database of personal information (such as a customer or employee database) is included in the target assets, ownership of the database will need to be transferred to the purchaser. As noted above, there is a specific exemption from the need to obtain the individual's consent to the transfer of information in the context of a business sale.

[540] In the context of either a share or asset sale, the purchaser should also ensure that any proposed expansion or changes to its use of personal information (including the sharing of personal information with any group companies) comply with the Privacy Act.

14.6 Anti-corruption, Anti-bribery and Anti-money Laundering

[541] Bribery and corruption are criminal offences in both the public and private sectors.

[542] The Crimes Act 1961 prohibits giving, receiving, accepting bribe (whether directly or indirectly) with the intent to influence a person's actions or omissions in an official capacity. This applies to public officials, such as members of Parliament, judges and police officers. It is also an offence to corruptly use official information or to trade a person's influence.

[543] The Secret Commissions Act 1910 prohibits giving, agreeing to, or offering an agent a gift or other form of consideration to induce or reward that agent's actions where this is done with a corrupt intention.

[544] In New Zealand, the Anti-Money Laundering and Countering Financing of Terrorism Act 2009 (the AML/CFT Act) governs AML requirements and offences. The AML/CFT Act prescribes requirements which reporting entities, including financial institutions, lawyers, bankers, real estate agents and similar professions, must follow when undertaking certain activities on behalf of their respective clients, including undertaking due diligence on their client and reporting suspicious transactions to the police.

www.ingramcontent.com/pod-product-compliance
Ingram Content Group UK Ltd.
Pitfield, Milton Keynes, MK11 3LW, UK
UKHW020149290926
15471UKWH00004B/776

9 789403 530222